Jessica Leichtweisz

Jessica Leichtweisz founded Hope Education Services in 2015 when she discovered that many parents around the world do not have access to the information they require to help their children affected by Autism.

By networking with parents, Autism professionals, and Autistic adults online, she noticed a big gap between how professionals coach parents of children with Autism and what Autistic adults have to say. For example, Jessica always taught parents to use person-first language while overwhelming, Autistic adults prefer identify-first language. Earlier in her career, she was dedicated to "recovering" children from Autism. Today, she is internationally acclaimed for using a behavioral approach that is centered not on making a child "less Autistic," but making sure Autism is not the reason for a person's suffering.

Jessica's mission is to make the world a more inclusive, loving and accepting place for everyone, including Autistic individuals. That's why she is committed to learning as much as she can about Autism directly from people experiencing it. Through her television show *Bridge the Gap*, weekly webinar *Ask and Autistic,* and now the book *This is Autism,* she is committed to helping parents and the community at large understand Autism better so mistakes of previous generations are not repeated and Autistic children have the best journey possible.

About the Compilers

Aidan Allman-Cooper

Aidan Allman-Cooper is the Founder and Chairman of SECA Organization LLC. A dynamic speaker and engaging presenter, Aidan has had multiple opportunities to discuss issues surrounding the special needs community in multiple venues. From conferences to seminars, Aidan is committed to serving the special needs community by relaying invaluable information regarding pertinent special education topics such as FAPE, IDEA, and the importance of IEP goals/objectives.

Prior to forming SECA, Aidan was a classified high school student at a public school. Ultimately, the challenges Aidan personally faced prompted him to become invested in ensuring the rights of special needs students are protected and that all students receive a Free and Appropriate Public Education.

Aidan has an intimate understanding of the special education process and regularly assists clients by reviewing IEPs and then attending meetings, consulting with school districts, mediating with schools, and providing overall effective assistance in whatever conflict you may be facing.

Aidan has a vested interest in compiling this book as he is not only sharing his own story of living with Autism, but he is especially dedicated to provide people with an insightful and raw look into what life is like living with Autism from a diverse variety of perspectives.

Forward

By Jessica Leichtweisz

I entered into the world of Autism in 2007. This was right at the heart of the Autism recovery movement. I had a bumper sticker on my car that said "Recovery is Possible." I went to Autism walks when they were still "walks for the cure" and encouraged parents to seek out "Defeat Autism Now" or "DAN" doctors.

I had some of the best applied behavior analysis (ABA) training available and truly believed that ABA could recover children from Autism forty percent of the time. Every time I worked with a child with Autism, my goal, no matter how severe it manifested for them, was to make them less Autistic.

It hadn't occurred to me that it was possible they didn't want to be less Autistic. It hadn't occurred to me that someone could be grateful for their Autism, celebrate it, and thrive with it.

It wasn't until almost a decade into my career that I had meaningfully interacted with Autistic adults. I worked with kids. Their parents got a diagnosis of Autism and they were afraid and confused. They didn't want their child to be Autistic. It meant their child was different than the person they thought they would. It meant financial sacrifices for therapies other parents didn't have to make. It meant there were things their child struggled with other kids didn't. It meant frustrations with behaviors and communication. To them, Autism was a bad thing and I just took that at face value.

I always knew kids with Autism grew up. I didn't really know what happened to them. I didn't give it much thought. I worked with them until they aged out of services. At that point, it was black and white to me. They either recovered and would live a "normal life" when they grew up, or they wouldn't and they would struggle. I really thought most adults with Autism either got better would never be fully independent.

I was wrong.

My purpose for being is to make the world a better place for people living with Autism. It is what ignites me. It gets me up in the morning and it is the last thing I think about when I go to bed. Every day, I pray asking God how I could best serve the Autistic community. I am so profoundly grateful to have found my purpose and for getting to live in it. How many people can truly say they love what they do?

I have made countless sacrifices skipping gym classes to write blog posts, create Youtube videos, or do consultations with parents on every continent, (except Antarctica). I was always happy to help. I put my mission of helping families affected by Autism before myself and it just came natural. I had such good intentions and thought I was doing things right.

Then, I started to get some negative reviews on my Facebook page written by Autistic adults. I was heartbroken and I didn't understand why. It would have been so easy to just dismiss them saying that they were Autistic and didn't know better. This was the moment in my life where it was hardest to put my mission before myself because it meant I had to take a good hard look at what I was doing and admit the possibility—I was making some mistakes.

I started to talk to Autistic adults. I found many differences between the way I perceived Autism and what I learned about Autism from other neurotypical professionals and how Autistic adults described their Autism. They taught me the difference between a tantrum and a meltdown, taught me why they stim and how vital it is to their wellbeing, and taught me that Autism acceptance is just as important as awareness.

When I first started working with kids with Autism, there was no unified adult Autistic community. Most Autistic adults lived spread apart and had no way of meeting each other. Social media changed everything in the best way possible. Today, there is a community of Autistic adults and they have valuable lessons, insights, and information to share.

Here are their stories.

Prologue

By Elizabeth D.

Running, full speed ahead, I stumble
Hair a mess and backpack overflowing
Just missed the bus
School was hell but I learnt to laugh...at myself
I confused my letters, reversed my words
Beginning to think my brain is scrambled
Like the last runner in a race
Lagging far behind the rest
And forever running to catch up
Cried a lot
But I'm not a quitter
Marching to the beat of a different drum
Found myself stuck in the funniest situations
I call it... Black Humor

Aidan Allman-Cooper

In addition to being a compiler, Aidan is pleased to be sharing his own story. Presented poignantly and raw, Aidan is detailing some of his experiences for the very first time. Aidan is excited to not only have others learn a little about his story, but is especially excited for others to read all of the submissions.

Chapter 1: "A Person's Journey"
By Aidan Allman-Cooper

Part I- The amount of joy that is felt when you watch a person's journey evolve in front of you is one that cannot be quantified. The feeling that I'm attempting to describe can and has been felt by many people. From parents watching their child's first ballet dance recital— to them watching their child performing at Madison Square Garden, or to the oncologist first beginning to treat the mother of four children with Stage III breast cancer and then watching her leave the hospital cancer-free, this feeling is truly one that is priceless. Fortunately, I have had the honor and privilege to experience this feeling not just on passing occasion, but on an actual frequent basis. Two years ago, I began my own personal journey into discovering what I was truly passionate about. It started off as a simple rebuttal to the expectations that were designated to people with special needs. To be more specific, the high school I went to unfortunately caused extreme distress to me and I found myself truly lost in a school where I felt my soul being evaporated each day as I entered the building. To them, I was the gay, Autistic, disabled kid with nothing to offer and nothing to gain from surrounding themselves with me. I witnessed the school's negative climate towards special needs students, through the physical violence and emotional abuse I endured, as well as witnessing it happen to others. I slowly began to remove myself from the toxic culture that was being perpetuated and accepted. Ultimately, I left my public high school after a lengthy emotionally-taxing battle and never in my life did I feel so helpless.

During this time, I was extremely sick with a rare condition called eosinophilic esophagitis and I also was diagnosed with ulcerative colitis. I was fighting against the constant physical pain, as well as the emotional pain that came with the ending of my career as a public school student. I pride myself on not being an angry person, as I tend to find that anger can often lead to wasted efforts and self-poisoning. Yet each day as I sat on my couch watching *Judge Judy* in my royal blue bathrobe, barely able to move, I was seething. How could a school and the students they produce treat someone in such a poor manner? Why did I have to be diagnosed with these diseases, coinciding with the concerns I had regarding my education?

The anger permeated through my entire being and almost took over my life. I became more hardened and less excited about the possibilities life could provide to me and the drive I used to feel evaporated. I had always wanted to be a teacher and a lawyer since I was a kid, as my goal was to help people, but the anger almost talked me out of following that vision I had for myself. I didn't believe in the beauty life or people had to offer and I began to conjure up several thoughts of disappointment. The trajectory of my life that I first thought of now consisted of me not pursuing teaching and law, rather, enduring an unexciting and uninspiring job at some office. Due to the lack of belief I had in humanity, even if I somehow was able to pull myself together and pursue teaching and law in the future, the monkey chatter in my mind still tried to convince me that I would always end up disappointed and uninspired. Fleeting thoughts of me sitting in a shoebox of an office reading stodgy real-estate transaction papers and occasionally teaching a class or two at the local high school—interacting with the brothers and sisters of the kids who used to make my life miserable and trying desperately to not have them be like their own siblings constantly crescendoed in my mind. Life was miserable and the constant physical and emotional pain I was in created an untenable environment that no one should have to endure. I remember reaching my breaking point quite well—the day I didn't care. I began a slow descent into not caring about anything around me, especially myself. The clothes I wore, the food I ate, the choices I made all seemed meaningless. The once dedicated and highly ambitious person I was morphed into this apathetic, angry, and miserable blob. It enraged me. I had to make a change—otherwise, I knew in due time, I would poison myself to no return.

The anger didn't go away overnight. It took some time for me to allow myself to let that self-destructive anger leave my soul, but I learned that I can still cling onto the anger that ignites my passion of serving others. I began researching everything I could about special education law, advocacy, parental/guardian rights, student rights, etc. The days once consumed of me sitting on the couch all day in my bathrobe watching *Judge Judy* turned into me wearing real clothes, still sitting on the couch most of the day, but instead of just watching television, I now had a purpose. I spent hours upon hours scouring the internet, self-teaching what struggles other special needs students face and what regulations are in place to help such students conquer these struggles—for I was captivated. Rather than allow myself to fall into a descent of unproductive misery, what if I was able to produce something positive? The drive slowly began to return and as I became more educated on disability law and hearing other stories of special needs students struggling, the anger returned. This time, however, this particular type of anger didn't poison my soul—it opened my soul up again. I was outraged at the atrocities I heard and the fact that many parents are trying their best to protect and help their disabled children but are instead given the run-around and are denied in various settings, particularly within schools. I became extremely curious and wondered if others had similar issues, such as the ones I experienced when I was in that particular school. My curiosity didn't just land to that one topic, for my curiosity extended to the overall nature of what types of struggles other special needs students had to deal with in my own community and what possible remedies were out there to help.

This intrigue led me to develop the Special Education Committee of Advocates, SECA. The goal at first was to start a conversation about the disenfranchisement of special needs individuals. I started to have community meetings at my local coffee shop and after a few sessions, I began to develop a small following. Concerned community members, mothers, fathers, and some students themselves began to inquire and even share more about their struggles and experiences within the education system. As I was having these sessions throughout the week, I would race onto my computer whenever I had a chance to dig up some archaic education case law or read articles written by parents and professionals on their perspectives on specific issues. I became more savvy and more aware of the issues impacting the special needs community and together with my small group, we began to demand change. Whether it was speaking at the local board of education meetings or organizing an awareness event, we were dedicated. In between this advocacy work, I began to wonder what would come about with my schooling.

With this invigoration, albeit still hesitant in some cases, I wanted to focus on earning my high school diploma. I remember visiting a preparatory school and then a therapeutic school and the feeling I had was rather ambivalent. Yes, it was probable that any of these schools would be much better than the public school. Still, I wasn't able to tell if it was my still-fleeting apathetic mindset in some areas or if it was just simply me not feeling excited about the schools themselves. All of that changed on one day—the day where my life changed forever.

I didn't know what type of school it was. Fusion Academy? Did it have something to do with a fusion of ideas? As soon as I walked into the building, the jittery feeling I had when I learned something new or when I was nervously-excited about the new book coming out returned. For the first time in what seemed like an endless amount of years, that excited feeling came back to me. Besides the purple-painted walls and beautifully-strung string lights, the people were the most attractive part. I couldn't fathom at how kind and conscientious they were. Would you like something to eat? Is there anything I could get you? It was so foreign to hear people, especially within a school, ask what they could do for me specifically. I was quite accustomed to being told what would happen to me at my past school and what roles I would have in my educational career, so I was completely dumbfounded. Nevertheless, I was able to answer the admission questions and was candidly honest about my experiences. I remember after the hour-long tour and meeting some of the students that I knew, definitely, that this was the place for me. I had a real chance this time! I was able to not be defined by my quirks and by the supposedly negative attributes that were designated towards me. I could even have friends that would celebrate my differences and want to hang out with me, rather than me occasionally saying hello to someone in the hallway while never looking into their eyes. So as soon as I walked into the director's office for the "private interview," I knew I had to nail it. But how? What would be something I could show her that would allow me admittance into this Eden? As they explained during the tour, they weren't a therapeutic school, rather, an alternative school for students both with/without disabilities looking for a fresh start. Maybe it was my imagination mixed together with anxiety, but it seemed that she was looking rather skeptical. I knew exactly why. My file! Highlighted, bolded, red-inked, painted, were the labels Major Depressive Disorder, Autistic Spectrum Disorder, and Post-Traumatic Stress Disorder. Yes, those labels were and are still accurate to this day. But I didn't want that to be a turn-off! On paper, those labels signify that the person may have a lot of baggage or areas to work on that would be best dealt within a private special education or therapeutic school. In other words, I felt she was probably thinking, "geez, this kid is going to be a piece of work." That's the problem with labels. Sure, they help with identifying some of the areas you need help with but in some instances, people may negatively react to them, intentionally or unintentionally. Despite my fear I wasn't going to be admitted, I somehow was able to charm her and assure her that despite the diagnoses, I was confident in my ability to grow and succeed as a person and student within Fusion Academy. When she finally broke the news that I would be accepted, tears flowed down my face and a handshake turning into a hug sealed the deal. I was officially going to be a Fusion student. This was the beginning of me reclaiming my life.

Part II-The days started to get brighter, literally. Spring had sprung and as I saw the sun shine more brightly, I began to see my spirits shine more brightly as well. Fusion was going great—I was learning how to make friends and was doing well academically. In fact, I created the Diversity Club and was engaged in various student activities throughout the day! In between school and clubs,

I was still incredibly busy back at home as I was still juggling the demands of SECA. At this point, I felt comfortable in providing advice to others. After constant research, review, studying, and conversations with people, I began to be recognized as someone who could provide valuable information. Questions ranging from how to get a child out of a public school into a private school, to what is the difference between an accommodation and a modification spammed my inbox on my laptop. The replying and working with parents and professionals consumed a large part of my time in conjunction with school responsibilities. I officially felt that I had gone from the barely moving couch potato to a relentless, newly re-inspired spirit.

Although I was satisfied for several months engaging in these aspects, I still felt I wanted more on both the school and professional end. I wanted to have more friends and more fun at school and on the business end, I wanted to serve more people and become more involved with educational advocacy and consulting. I soon began to take more chances at school through the support of teachers and fellow classmates. Attending school dances and going on field trips became possible through the compassion that was extended to me. I also was able to accelerate academically and because of my reignited passion in education, I was even able to graduate high school early in November of 2019. This newly risky side of me wasn't just seen in school—I began to take some risks on the professional side as well.

As more and more people began to ask for my guidance on certain educational issues, I began to think I could make a more positive difference to the community. Instead of doing this advocacy work on the side, what if I could make it into a form of self-employment? Using my trusty computer, I found LegalZoom, filed the LLC papers, got it approved, and a few weeks after filing, I became an official business in January of 2020! A new business, a new high school graduate, but what could I personally do to serve more people? I had a lot of unoccupied time and wanted to be as productive as possible—I didn't want to go back to that apathetic self I had previously. I also knew that if I was going to create a business, the charitable spirit that SECA was should carry into SECA LLC.

After signing the leasing agreement, I moved in March of 2020. Due to the pro-bono clinic I created along with price-reduced consulting services, I've been fortunate enough to serve many low-income families and students. Recall earlier, I described that feeling of joy when watching someone's personal journey evolve. The best part of my life is that despite the odds against me, I was able to somehow find a profession that I'm not only able to feel passionate about, but that I'm able to frequently experience that wonderful feeling. The amazing stories I've heard and people I've worked with have allowed me to see a person grow and evolve.

I remember one of the first cases I worked on where I really experienced that indescribable feeling. A 14 year old with ADHD was having extreme behavioral and academic issues at his school and was in a downward spiral. I remember first meeting him in my office and being cursed and screamed at by him, as he exclaimed the stupidity of the people at his school and how much he hates his classes. Now on the surface, it appears that this is just an angry young man with some behavioral and academic issues. After learning more about his own journey thus far through conversing with him and through his mother, I learned the non-label part of him. Going deeper into where some of the anger stems from, I later learn that his father was incarcerated and wasn't present for the entirety of his childhood, was at one point on the verge of homelessness, and was mercilessly bullied by fellow classmates his entire educational career. Hearing his journey as an individual thus far was hard to hear—seeing him squirm in the chair and hearing his voice crack and tears enter into his eyes when he describes the bullying. It was imperative for me to learn more about the challenges and experiences he went through as that would allow me to connect his current actions and behaviors to some of the feelings he was expressing to me. From there, I would be able to design an action plan and work with his mother on his educational programming. But I needed to know more about his passions and what, if any, aspects in his life brought him joy.

I quickly found out that he is infatuated with anything car-related. I saw a grin break out on his face as he told me all of his favorite cars, what type of horsepower they have, when they were made, and other facets of the cars. Finding a passion reclaimed my life—that could easily occur for him as well. He needed to not only find something to be excited about in his personal life, but to also feel capable both emotionally and academically to succeed. After a lengthy battle with his public school district followed by a series of court hearings, an agreement was eventually reached in which the district would compensate for at least a year of educational services in a therapeutic school and will evaluate his needs each year determining whether he still requires the out of district placement.

Since then, he has been doing better academically at this school, has not been bullied by his new classmates, and has had a significant decrease in meltdowns since being at the school. Outside of school, he is flourishing as well and currently is in a Go-Kart club with a few of his friends and works part-time at an auto-body shop. In fact, I recently obtained a car and took it to his body shop to say hello! The joy I saw in his eyes and the large smile he had as he looked over my car and chatted with me is the feeling I described. A year and a half ago, he was an angry out of control kid with severe behavioral issues and academic concerns and since then, he has been able to reclaim his life.

I mention this case to point to the awesome pleasure of seeing a person evolve in front of your eyes. Being able to know that you were able to help someone reach their immense potential and to have a revelation that there is a better way to approach life is what keeps me going.

Through my own experiences, I have learned to approach life in a much different way and being able to express what I've learned to others who may be in a similar situation feels surreal. In the course of doing advocacy work, I've unfortunately had cases where positive results were not met. One such case was when I had a 16 year old teenage girl who was sexually abused as a girl and had bipolar disorder, who refused to take her medication. I remember meeting her grandmother and looking into her desperate eyes, begging me to help her daughter. I did everything I could in that particular case and for a while, she seemed to be improving. However, I was then told that she was arrested for vandalism and assault and was later put on house arrest. The last I've heard from her was her cutting off her ankle monitor and attempting to flee New Jersey. Currently, she's being housed in a juvenile detention facility.

There have been so many heart-wrenching and brutal stories and many of them make me want to reconsider careers. I'm haunted by the stories and am even more haunted by the fact that perhaps if I did something else, different results may have occurred. Despite this, I've had to learn the harsh reality that I'm unable to help everyone and that you can't allow yourself to be swallowed alive by the stories. Instead of succumbing to negativity, I choose to celebrate the victories that occur and the lessons I learn from each case. It may sound odd, but I am in a small way, grateful for what happened to me for if I didn't endure the traumatic experiences, I wouldn't have had the involvement in one of the most considerable pleasures in all of life—watching a live human being morph from a caterpillar into a butterfly. I sincerely hope that in my own journey, I'm slowly beginning to turn into a butterfly.

Part III-The past few months have been an absolute whirlwind. With an influx of cases I'm managing, it's been hard to keep afloat. My life had become even more arduous when I realized I would launch into one of the biggest challenges of my life—compiling and writing a book.

It had always been a childhood dream of mine to write. In fact, my mother named me Aidan James as she said it sounded like "an author's name." I always knew I would write at least one book before the end of my life—that was my lifetime goal. I never realized that Jessica and I would not only compile it within a month, but have me personally write about some of the most vulnerable things about myself. From the start of this endeavor, our goal was simple. We wanted to create an anthology series highlighting the lessons, values, experiences, obstacles, and perspectives from Autistic adults.

As I described previously, I've not only had experiences in which I was treated unfairly due to my disability, but I've also seen it firsthand as an advocate. If there could be one takeaway from this book, my goal would be that not only does Autism appear differently in others, but there is a sense of unique beauty displayed in everyone with Autism. Whether they find their Autism to be a hindrance or a sincere asset is each person's prerogative and there is no wrong way in expressing that. As you read all of our stories, there is one conclusion that I believe is definite—there is a common factor in that there is such diverse beauty among us.

Far too often, people with Autism are often invalidated and are told that their "perception is off" or that they need to "put themselves in someone else's shoes." We are told to learn the neurotypical ways in socializing, communicating, and behaving. While I find it incredibly imperative that people with Autism learn important skills such as socializing or communicating as there may exist a deficiency in that area, the assets as well as the difficulties of having Autism are overlooked. This is an opportunity for you to hear from Autistic adults themselves and what life is really like for them, in addition to both the skills they've either learned or are beginning to absorb and areas that did or still do signify difficulty.

At the end of the day, what matters most is that more people are aware of the humanity and the richness that is found within the Autisic community as well as the perspectives that people with Autism may have. With that being said, I will attempt to describe what it is like living with Autism.

To me, there is no simple answer. Some people may perhaps expect a simple response such as "it's hard sometimes, but I manage." The truth is that there really is no simple response you can give. In fact, I find my Autism rather enigmatic, but I do agree with the response of "it's hard sometimes, but I manage." Frequently due to my insecurity in addition to fear of coming off as pedantic as I explain the depths of my Autism, I would muddle that simple response. This may be due to a growth of self-confidence, but I've been less sensitive and more willing to candidly discuss what life is like living with Autism.

To me, having Autism is both a blessing and a curse. To start on the negative sides, I will be honest and admit how lonely it can get for me. I have an incredibly challenging time in making friends, as anxiety paralyzes me in what I like to say "going to the next level." While I've been able to master etiquette skills and am able to not come across as socially awkward, I still find myself unable to elevate friendships. Due to past trauma as well as a lacking self-esteem, the concept of me being unlikeable and unlovable has been a substantial force in preventing me from moving forward with relationships. Where Autism comes in is the rather perseverative thinking I have. Fleeting thoughts are constant as I ponder whether or not I matter to people or if people would actually want to spend time with me or even love me.

Besides the difficulty in making friends and the negative perseverative thinking, I would have to say that one of the most challenging aspects of having Autism is the rejection that comes from it. Unfortunately, some people I have had the opportunity to interact with have mocked the way I occasionally stutter or stammer my words, in addition to how I communicate with people. In the past, I used to try and elevate friendships and be more social, but the names I've been called due to some of the effects of me having Autism is devastating. I've wanted to stop socializing altogether due to these negative experiences as well as protecting myself from rejection.

Additionally, it gets extremely exhausting not always understanding if people are laughing with or at you and it becomes extremely emotionally taxing in trying to find that out. On the opposite end of my Autism being challenging at times, there are many positive qualities that are offered. For one thing, I feel as though I have a high level of insight which allows me to identify some of the strengths and areas on what I would like to improve on myself. This insight isn't just garnered to me, but rather, I feel as though I have a higher level of insight on others as well. As I previously mentioned, I did not want to socialize with anyone due to my negative experiences. Due to the insight my Autism provides to me, I have also looked into the values that other people have that may contrast with my own. For example, I would sometimes see myself trying to be friends with people who aren't necessarily interested in me, but I would vehemently do so just to say that I have a friend. As I've gotten older, the increase of recognizing such individuals has allowed me to gravitate to people who are non-judgemental, kind, and actually those who are interested in me as a person. I'm starting to learn that I matter, and the values I have are actually shared by others as well.

This revelation has slowly changed my life as I've been able to socialize with more people recently and have actually developed positive friendships. I will be honest and admit that life today still is not perfect. I still am in physical pain and find it hard to feel happy overall. I also know that I will always have Autism and challenges associated with it. However, I also recognize that there will always be strengths.

I am a compassionate person who has a lot of love to give towards others, in addition to my drive to change the world. Autism reinforces those values due to the perseverative thinking as well as the understanding of rejection. Due to the positive values I find myself possessing, I can conclusively say with conviction that I would not rid myself of Autism if I had the opportunity to do so.

As you read other contributors' stories, I invite you to open your mind and heart in learning more about various perspectives from other Autistic individuals, as well as the immense courage they have in sharing their stories and thoughts. By listening, asking questions, opening your mind, and accepting others, we can make a better tomorrow.

RACHEL HAWKINS

Rachel Hawkins is both an Occupational Therapist and a self-advocate for Autism. She seeks to inspire others to accept and love who they are, with all their strengths and weaknesses combined. Rachel graduated from Goucher College with a bachelor's degree in political science and got her master's degree in occupational therapy from Temple University. She now lives in Northern Virginia with her husband and teenage stepdaughter. She enjoys traveling, music, photography and being creative during her free time. Most recently, Rachel developed *Transition to Independence: Unlocking Special Abilities*, a curriculum for young adults with various "special abilities" to learn and practice independent living and vocational skills. She has developed a presentation "Variety is the Spice of Work" and appeared on multiple interview platforms from podcasts to YouTube videos, and is incredibly excited to share her story on those various mediums. She is inspired to use her personal and professional experiences to speak about being an advocate and inclusion for all individuals, regardless of ability or difference.

Chapter 2: "Through Adversity Comes Strength"

By Rachel Hawkins

As an occupational therapist and a self-advocate for Autism, I have a unique position to speak about my experience. I have been on both sides of the therapist/patient relationship and feel this gives me an edge in work settings. Growing up in the 1980's was challenging as there was almost nothing known of Autism. I was seen as different and did not "fit in." In a sense, I had a very difficult childhood, but I would not trade it for anything because of the lessons and values I grew to adopt.

Lesson 1: Cultivate an Individual's Talents

Unbeknownst to my parents, music became a major influence in my life. I started Suzuki violin at three years old as my mom learned that it supposedly helped develop brain activity and development. Within a few years, I switched to piano. I have a talent for playing by ear. After my violin lesson, I would run upstairs in the church building where my lessons were held and play the same song on the piano. My grandparents bought me a piano and I took lessons throughout my school years and continued playing through college. To this day, I am involved with music and play on occasion. I would still love to be part of a jazz group that performs.

Piano remained my main instrument, although I started flute in 4th grade and returned to violin in high school. Throughout my life, I have tried other instruments and am still interested in learning more. My parents bought me an acoustic guitar one year for a present, again as a way to make friends because when people sit around, someone like me would strum the guitar for a sing along. I could never figure out the chords on a guitar, though, and found bass much easier. I tried clarinet once at summer camp along with drums, and upright bass in college. I had taken electric bass lessons at summer camp, but this was not offered at my college, so I lugged around the upright bass to the music department from my dorm room for lessons.

What music provided me was an equal playing field. I was able to express myself without talking. Especially in jazz, one needs to listen to the other instrumentalists or vocalists and nonverbally communicate the order of solos or when to trade 4's. I found myself looking at my band mates and giving a small head nod, for example. Not everything in jazz is rehearsed except the "head" of a tune, as solos change each time the song is played. However, unlike conversation, once someone begins a solo, there is no interruption until that player is finished and the process begins again with another.

I can't say for sure if this helped me in actual conversations, but it allowed me to express myself creatively. There was a sense of belonging when I participated in band, orchestra, or jazz ensemble. I have always enjoyed performing and still love to be in front of people whether playing music or giving a speech.

Lesson 2: With Our Weaknesses Come Strong Assets

I always learned best visually and was weak with verbal interaction and memory. In elementary school and early childhood, I was fascinated with letters and was an avid reader. In school, it was hard to listen to a lecture and take notes from it. Reading comprehension was a challenge. I still have trouble making an image of what I am reading, like imagining what characters look like. During my senior year of high school, I enrolled in a Lindamood-Bell program in which I learned to make pictures from what I was reading, and it did help my comprehension. In college and graduate school, I was much better at listening to lectures and taking notes.

My sensory issues were much more extreme as a young child. My mother tells me she cut out all of the tags in my t-shirts because I would complain that the tags irritated my skin. I still have eczema and sensitive skin. In fact, if I am in the sun for a short time I develop a rash, so I wear long sleeve shirts to prevent this. Now they make tagless clothing! Imagine if that had been available back when I was growing up. Every night before bed, I would ask "Will there be any lightning, thunder, and rain tonight?" The loud noises startled me, and to this day I experience thunder as extremely loud. But I had many more sensitivities to noise—the vacuum, toilet flushing, hand dryers, etc. Again, if I had grown up in the current society, there would be many more modifications available.

At 13-14, my mom found a clinic in Darien, Connecticut that had Auditory Integration Training, which was said to decrease sensitivities to sounds and normalize the reaction to stimuli. We traveled there for 10 days, and I listened to distorted music through headphones twice a day, morning and afternoon. Our entertainment consisted of shopping and eating at the local restaurants. This was a big help even to my sense of touch as I believe it helped normalize my sensory systems in general.

Performing and public speaking were always easy for me. When you're playing an instrument or doing a speech, everything is rehearsed and prepared. You practice it ahead of time. I was comfortable knowing what I was going to say without any interruptions or spontaneous comments. However, when I was talking to someone, especially multiple people, I had to judge when to interject my comment and figure out what to say that related to the conversation, all while making eye contact and expressing nonverbally my message.

I always did very well academically, but I struggled socially in school. It was hard to make friends and kids picked up that I was "different" and did not make my experience easy. My parents put me in all kinds of activities growing up, I think to see which would stick. From Girl Scouts to martial arts, I did it all including all kinds of therapies to try to "fix" what my parents, (and I), perceived as wrong.

At one of my first summers at an overnight camp, Bucks Rock Performing Arts Camp, my bunkmates confided in a counselor that I was not talking to them. As the story was told to me, this counselor has two children, one being dyslexic and one being hyperlexic. She shared with my parents this information and suggested that maybe I was hyperlexic and things started to make sense. Hyperlexia is defined as an advanced reading ability and fascination with letters and numbers. I was always a very good reader and writer but did not express myself well verbally. Around the time of July 4, my dad made me a little letter with checkboxes to help me "declare my independence." as we were just starting to understand why I was the way I am. In my recollection, it read something like:

I do better with written material.

Yes

No

It was at this camp that I made more close friends in the years to come—getting involved with unique activities such as woodworking, improv, (comedy), and dabbling in glassblowing, jewelry making, and batik, among others. I performed in the improv show and did well in that because of the rules involved. The rules are easy because you make statements and go along with whatever your partner(s) suggest, (yes, and). This means if they say you are brother and sister, you expand on that. I got to try tap dance and of course participated in the orchestra and jazz band. I became a CIT, (Counselor in Training), in music and wood shop and then a junior counselor in music. I remember learning how to play cricket and playing soccer, (football), with the counselors from the UK and Australia, and evening activities like "capture the flag."

For years when I would go out with my parents, I admired my dad's ability to talk to anyone. He would just strike up a conversation with someone sitting near him at the bar and have fun with the person laughing and being playful. I always said, "I wish I could be like that." In my childhood and teen years, this was extremely hard for me and I didn't realize I had the skills to do this. Now that I'm all grown up, I realize this is not an innate ability but one that can be developed, and I now find myself doing the same thing.

We understand, though we may not respond. I always understood what was going on around me. I felt rejected when my "friends" said "you can't be our friend anymore." Of course, I had no idea what I had done, and now realize it meant more about them than me. I always said I had empathy and felt strong emotions, although I do not always express them like neurotypical people do. I still have never cried at a movie. I feel emotions internally, but it can be hard to express them so that others understand them.

It was patronizing when certain therapists spoke to me by relating to my "disability," versus me as a person. They seemed to disregard my skills and worked to correct my problems. It seemed that no professional really sided with me and my experience, but there was one exception. I received outpatient speech therapy with Mrs. Hammond, who I think really understood me and my differences. She not only made it fun, but she related to me on a personal level. We would go to the mall and try to figure out how people were related by how they walked together. Were they holding hands and the same age? Probably a couple. Was it an older man and a young girl? Father and daughter.

Lesson 3: Find the Best Fit for Your Child

Due to my sensory issues and lack of social connection, moving me to a small private boarding and day high school was a good decision. I attended a school 45 minutes to one hour away from my home, but instead of a graduating class of about 1,300 students, my graduating class had thirty. I was known at this school by my teachers and my peers.

As this was a college preparatory school, I found the students were taking the classes more seriously than in the large public school. My classmates in public school would talk throughout class, which was very distracting to me, especially given my auditory sensitivities. It was much harder to communicate and relate to my classmates at such large schools.

I participated in extracurricular activities such as lacrosse, soccer, and rock climbing, and took courses on logic and debate. I had a few close friends, although it was hard to make plans because I lived so far away. My classes were engaging and fun, and the other students seemed interested in learning as well.

Some students at this school came from foreign countries such as Germany and Japan. There was a conversation partner program, in which students were paired up one-on-one with a student from another country. I was encouraged to participate in this program because my parents and teachers felt it would be beneficial for my communication skills. I think in some ways my partners were better at social conversation than I was, but it allowed me another opportunity to connect.

It made sense that I also looked at smaller colleges. My parents and I visited some in Massachusetts, Connecticut, and Goucher College in Maryland, where I ended up going. I felt the others were too far away, and the school was a good size for me with about 1,200 students. I have always said that for my first couple of years, it was a good size, but by the time my junior and senior year hit, it felt small. It was comforting to be so close to home, only about a two-hour drive, and in hindsight, this was easier for my parents who drove me back and forth before and after breaks.

I participated in the jazz ensemble all four years and had various friends and would walk into town for dinner or shopping. We would visit Baltimore at times. I participated with the political groups and traveled to South Dakota to campaign for Senator Tim Johnson, who won by only ~500 votes. I interned in DC and thoroughly enjoyed my time on Capitol Hill and experiencing all that the city had to offer.

I never hesitated to participate in activities, despite my social challenges. For my study abroad, I chose to do a program connected with Tulane University and spent a summer in London studying international and comparative politics. I was able to relate well to the other five students as well as the group we met from Worcester Polytechnic Institute. I also connected with some business associates of my dad and extended family. I had no problem exploring the city on my own as well as taking pictures or shopping.

However, one day, I noticed my backpack had been opened and my things were moved. I talked to my roommate about this as I had kept a journal in my bag. She denied looking in my bag, but I knew someone must have been looking through my items. In hindsight, it was probably because I did not share much with the other students and she was trying to get to know what was going on with me. Of course, if we knew then what we know now, I would have been able to express myself and who I am to create a level of understanding.

Lesson 4: Find Others for Support

It was during these years that my parents got involved with support groups for Autism. They learned more about what being on the spectrum meant and were featured in a *New York Times* article. I attended some Autism conferences with them and was introduced to other advocates with whom I have since developed relationships. My dad told me about a major point discussed in one session he attended. Why don't we teach everyone else about those who are different? Why not put the onus on everyone else to adapt to those who are "disabled/different?"

Looking back, my college being a liberal arts school, there were students who did not fit into the "norm." My high school was the same way, as was the summer camp I attended. This was no accident, as my parents sought environments for me that they thought would work best. Maybe this is one reason I fit in so well in these places. It was in college I started to realize how I impact others being on the spectrum. My close friend read the *New York Times* article featuring my parents and related to being on the spectrum herself.

After college graduation, a major medical emergency put my uncertain plans on hold, and this is what led to my eventual career in occupational therapy. However, my initial drive and motivation for the field of occupational therapy was not due to being on the Autism spectrum. Being impacted physically, I received physical therapy in the hospital and outpatient setting. I learned to walk again using a walker, (the cane was too unsteady), and relearned to do the most basic tasks (ADL-Activities of Daily Living). I realized that during this time, an occupational therapist would be the one to help with washing my hair and putting on my shirt, two things I remember having trouble doing. I thought this would be a wonderful career where I could make a difference, and as put at a national conference, a career where "science, creativity, and compassion collide." Since I am strong in all of those things, it seemed like a perfect field for me. My parents were both self-employed and able to take time off of work to help me in whatever way they could, so I did not require in-home services. The physical therapists did a great job of working on my strength and range of motion, so that I am now able to run and do everything like I did before my injury.

Lesson 5: Patience is a Virtue

When I was strong enough to walk on my own and regained most of my independence, I worked part time at Starbucks and took prerequisites to apply for graduate school. I saw my survival as my second chance at life and vowed to come back stronger than ever.

In graduate school I lived in Center City, Philadelphia in my own apartment and this was the first time in my life I had a group of girlfriends. We all got together and went out to bars or clubs, or got together at each other's apartments. At each level of education, I felt better able to interact socially, although my skills did affect my ability to interact with patients in my fieldwork settings. The only area I got marked lower in was social interaction, and this caused me to repeat a fieldwork experience. Again, I felt discouraged because I was not performing at the level the rest of my class was. I have found that with the right supervisor and placement, however, I was able to be successful and have since learned to fully accept myself. When I disclosed my Autism or difficulty with social skills, it made it easier to navigate the work setting. There was more understanding and accommodation.

I always liked learning about psychological disorders growing up and would read about them in my teen magazines. One of my favorite fieldwork experiences was working at the inpatient psychiatric unit at Pennsylvania Hospital. I was able to connect with my supervisor and certain patients pretty easily. I led group sessions and most of the activities were arts and crafts, games, or group meetings. Looking back, maybe this is because my mind is wired differently just like theirs and there is an unspoken connection.

Lesson 6: Know Yourself and Appreciate Who You Are

Over the past 10 years, I have worked in mostly contractual jobs in the school setting. My most recent job and the one before that were my favorites, due to my job description and my coworkers. With both I was upfront about my being on the spectrum, and I explained that this allowed me to put myself literally in the student's/client's shoes, because I had been there before. I know what it is like for the family. I can see what life was like for my parents having a child who struggled with social relationships as well as sensory issues and expressive language difficulties.

What works for me in a job is consistency and predictability, with supervisors who see me for my ability and work with me to be successful. Being on the spectrum, I have a quiet strength that I can use in my interactions with clients. Most therapists in the pediatric setting are more of a "Rah! Rah! Cheerleader," and have an ability to connect with people immediately. I've found that my being on the spectrum allows me to connect with my clients in a different way, and with explanation, it puts families' minds at ease about my abilities. Also, I am better at working with older children or young adults because I can have conversations with them, versus young children who need much more excitement and expression.

A part of me still did not want to accept my challenges with connecting to others. I hid my Autism from my supervisors and coworkers because I felt it shouldn't be an issue and I should be able to overcome it. I found out, quickly, that this would not work.

When I am upfront about my differences even though people may still have difficulty understanding me, they know why I may not connect to their child and themselves. I also realize it is nothing to hide, because my Autism makes me the person I am. My last supervisors told me about the big change they saw in my ability to express myself even in my interview. I created my job as Director of Transition to Independence, in which I initiated programming for young adults to learn skills to be independent. The other component was working with companies to improve or start neurodiverse hiring programs or expanding their knowledge of neurodiversity in general to make their company more productive and attractive.

Advocacy

Throughout my life, I have been part of self-advocacy groups, including the Pennsylvania Autism Self Advocacy Network. It was with this group that I first presented my experience to support staff who work directly with those on the spectrum. I attended the Penn State Autism Conference, met parents of children on the spectrum, and came across people such as Scott Robertson for the first time. While I stopped attending conferences and participating in advocacy work at this time, my passion would return years later...

In May of 2019, I attended the Autism Symposium, hosted by SAP and the Philadelphia Eagles. Held at Lincoln Financial Field, executives from major companies spoke about their neurodiverse hiring programs. SAP, Wawa, The Precisionists, and more took questions in a panel format about how they got started and what the programs look like. To support me, my dad also attended, and we both found it enlightening and inspiring. My dad is a season ticket holder for the Eagles and passionate about the success of his children.

Since this event, I have connected with the Autism at Work Capital Region group here in DC and attended the kickoff meetings. I am now looking to use my personal and professional skills where I can impact a company's diversity and inclusion by offering a unique perspective. As someone who has lived the experience and worked with others, I can offer something others are unable to from the perspective of those affected by office spaces and office politics.

So what now? I seek to educate parents, other professionals, and educators on my experience and how to best relate to those with Autism. Looking back on my life, I have learned the hard way and wish people had a better understanding of what my experience was like. I think in today's society, there is much more knowledge and research being done with a long way to go. Self-advocates need to be included in the conversation and make changes that will impact us as we have a tremendous amount to offer.

Personal Life

For years, I did not understand dating or flirting. I still don't. My mom encouraged me to walk a particular way or give certain looks to be flirtatious, but I always was just being myself. I had never had a significant romantic relationship until meeting the man who became my husband. My parents always encouraged me to explore various avenues for meeting people, most of which I did online.

In college I had a few friends who showed interest in me, but I was not interested in them romantically. It was also awkward for me to have guys show interest because that was new. However, we remained friends throughout our years at college. In graduate school, again, I tried online dating with no success. It was not until I moved to Virginia for work that I would meet the love of my life.

My grandmother always said, "It only takes one." She meant that you don't need to date many people or have a lot of experience, you only need to meet the right person. Six years ago, at a match.com event, I met my (now) husband. I did not know this at the time, because I hardly interacted with him at the event.

The day after this event, which was a cooking class, he emailed me through the match.com site with a creative email. It was not the traditional message I would receive through an online dating platform. I responded, and soon after we set up our first date. About a week after the initial event, I met him at Ruth Chris Steak House in Bethesda, Maryland. We planned to attend a swing dance at Glen

Echo park after dinner, but that was closed due to the government shutdown at that time, so we just sat and talked inside a hotel lobby for a few hours. This was the first time I really felt a connection and was comfortable with a guy, and the next day we had our second date.

On the second date, I met his daughter and a few weeks later would go with them to King's Dominion (an amusement park) just because I wanted to spend more time with him. I invited him to my birthday dinner with my parents outside of Philadelphia, and we drove up to meet them. It all happened very fast, but I knew I met a good person and someone I was very interested in getting to know more. Since then, I had moved in with him and later we bought our first house together. We just celebrated our 4th anniversary and I am excited to be planning our 5th wedding anniversary for next summer.

Miscellaneous Thoughts

Our "obsessions" are just intense interests. Why is it an obsession for an autistic person but an interest for a neurotypical person? We should channel these interests into a possible career or an activity, where the person can make connections and excel. Also, not all Autistic people are good at math and computers. I am a good example of that. I never liked math, although I did do well in the sciences as evidenced by my profession. While the stereotype Autistic person likes train timetables, everyone is different.

Trial and error. Sometimes this is what it takes to determine an individual's interest or skill. My parents put me in pretty much everything they could think of including aikido, Girl Scouts, summer camp, music, theater, soccer, softball, along with speech therapy, occupational therapy, psychology and psychiatry. With no information available in the 1980's and 1990's, my parents got me involved in many activities, I think to see which would stick. As stated before, music stuck with me due to my parents' efforts to get me involved in a variety of activities and groups.

Put some of the onus on neurotypicals. Social interaction is very difficult for those on the spectrum. Why put all of the responsibility on us to create connections and follow all the rules? The rules don't even make sense to us. Education starts at home and I would encourage parents to teach their children about differences in people and how to be accepting.

Take a chance on us and utilize our skills. There are many Autism hiring programs in more and more companies today. This is successful because those on the spectrum bring their unusual perspectives and are seen in a positive light for what they offer. Accommodations made for individuals on the autism spectrum can really work for everyone. This is the principle of universal design. For example, open workspaces are a drawback for many people due to the distractions and overwhelming light.

Autistic vs "have autism"? This is a lesson I myself learned recently. Not all self-advocates refer to having autism or being on the spectrum, but rather that they are autistic. We need to recognize how each person refers to themselves. I have always felt comfortable saying I am on the spectrum

or have autism, and recently the stigma of saying I am
autistic has worn off slightly.

Sarina Black

Sarina currently works as a freelance designer, and lives with her partner and two children. After discovering she was Autistic in 2019, shortly before turning 32, Sarina began to spend a lot of time learning from the online Autistic community and found it to be incredibly supportive, especially for late-diagnosed adults. In June 2020, Sarina created her own Instagram blog to share her own experiences to help build community support, acceptance, and awareness.

Chapter 3: "Revelations Later On"
By Sarina Black

Sometimes I wonder how my life would have been different for me if I had known sooner that I am Autistic. I didn't find out until I was almost 32 years old, after having children of my own! For me, being Autistic has meant having a life that is more sensitive, more unique, and also more complex than most. Some days, that is easy for me to accept or even appreciate, and some days it isn't. Up until very recently, the general scope on how Autism looks was very limited. Now, we are finding out there are more and more of us all around, and we are connecting with each other. We come in every look, age, and background. I am so incredibly excited for what acceptance and awareness will bring for the next generations, especially when given the chance to thrive.

From my earliest memory, (which started at around 6 months), I have always known that I was different than most people around me. I played differently, but I was also an only child when I was young, so I was good at playing by myself. Looking back, a lot of the "different" ways I played have arguably become useful to me now in life, for example, I loved cars, (real and toys), and my favorite way to play with them was with a floor mat that had a city road design layout. I loved driving my cars on it and especially parallel parking them. When I got older and started playing video games, I loved to play racing games the wrong way and just try to drive realistically, (even Mario Kart). I am now an adept driver with a very good sense of spatial awareness with my vehicle, and yes, I still enjoy parallel parking!

As I grew up, the feelings of being different were only amplified more and more. I didn't care much for being around people my age because we weren't interested in the same things. I was always "too serious," which is a label that has followed me my entire life. I remember one year when I was invited to my friend's birthday party, at the start of the party I was excited, then when the kids all decided to move to another room in the house, I stayed behind and asked the parents if I could just stay and hang out with them. I never even thought at the time that maybe that was strange to do, but I did know that I had no interest in spending more time with my peers. It's not that I felt older or more mature than them, I just felt completely different. Alien, almost. But I never actually felt bad about myself or wished I was different, although I definitely felt bad about situations I wished were different. Mostly, I just wished I was received better and wished I knew why things that seemed easy for everyone else were almost impossible for me.

As an adult, I had experienced a few times of finding certain things that pointed to me being Autistic, but I didn't think it was possible to have gotten so far in my life without knowing. It wasn't until I had my first child and started reading about signs of Autism in children that I then realized most of the things I was seeing mentioned were things I thought seemed completely natural and ordinary and usually something I remembered doing from my own childhood. I started reading online, reading other experiences of Autistics, and even took some online quizzes. Once I unlearned the small range of stereotypes I had known of autism, I quickly realized without a doubt that I was Autistic and decided to pursue an official answer. If only I had been able to do this a little sooner, maybe I could have prevented my worst burnout period also by better advocating for my needs earlier on.

Jobs and the workplace is a mostly unavoidable

place that can be unbearable for Autistics. Of course, all Autistics are different just like any other person, but generally speaking, the environments are not usually healthy. Harsh lighting is frequently used, such as fluorescent lighting, which can be physically painful for us Autistics with sensory processing disorder. I used to routinely get physically sick from my jobs because of the lighting alone, spending my days on pain relievers and frequent bathroom visits. Smells, neighboring noises, and close quarters are also common contributions to difficult work settings. My most common personal criticism at every job has been my lack of socialization because I would prefer to eat my lunch alone, (this served as a quick way to recharge during the day when I couldn't get a break), or I would prefer to take a walk around outside alone instead of join in on team games during lunch. Inside the job role, I have always performed well and been reliable, with managers raving about my high performance compared to other employees. But the impossible social demands that come along with most workplaces is what can mean the difference of whether a job is able to be held by an Autistic.

Both workplaces and social settings have been a

common grounds of misunderstandings for myself because it's where I've encountered the most situations where my actions or facial expressions were misread. Autistics are no stranger to being misunderstood or having communication troubles, partly because some of us have a difficult time with appropriate facial expressions, (the type of expression, the amount of the expression, all of it). I have on numerous occasions been enjoying something immensely only to be interrupted by someone concerned about why I'm miserable, or made a new friend and then later learned they were scared of me when we first met. This type of feedback can be really upsetting to hear when it's completely untrue, and usually makes me feel embarrassed and confused. Trying to avoid these situations has led to me spending countless collective hours practicing facial expressions, trying to memorize how to use it, just to avoid these hurtful misunderstandings. Along with misinterpreted facial expressions, many, many times I have been accused of being under the influence of substances because of difficulty speaking or because of physical coordination issues. I have been accused of lying because I have a difficult time with eye contact and I am no stranger to being treated suspiciously in stores because I want to be alone and am probably wearing sunglasses. While these things can cause a negative situation for me, they also can't be helped, and trying to avoid them for years can contribute to an Autistic burnout.

Autistic burnout is something that is a fairly new topic in the medical field, but it's nothing new to Autistics. When someone experiences Autistic burnout, it is not uncommon for them to seemingly crash completely. Skills may be lost and may not always be recovered completely. Things like constant masking contribute to this and also things like being in unhealthy circumstances for too long with no recharge. It is thought that burnouts tend to coincide with peak age points, usually in conjunction with major life transition points such as puberty or moving out. I experienced my first burnout at around the age of 12 when I was experiencing a myriad of transitions everywhere in my life. My grandparents immigrated from Iran and moved into our small mobile home. I was experiencing friend troubles and felt abandoned by my closest friends as I felt the divide between my interests suddenly being seen as immature. I was having trouble focusing on school. Eventually, this all manifested into a burnout that was eventually called depression, but it wasn't that. I had trouble swallowing my food for about a year because I developed anxiety over how to swallow. I did not want to go to any of my activities or see anyone I knew. All of the things that were soothing to me, like rocking (movement) or listening to music on headphones, (helpful in sensory overload), were either called too weird or I was told I was being a rude teenager. This is a time when I wish I had known I was Autistic then, because both myself and my parents would have known it was okay to need those things and that I wasn't being bad or trying to rebel.

I have since had two more identifiable burnout periods, next at around the age of 18 and then just after 30. I spent my 20's no longer trying as hard to figure out what was different about me and remained more focused on how to blend in so I finally would not be such a target for some things or people. In many ways, I am still recovering from my last burnout even years later, partly because of how hard it hit but mostly because initially, I didn't know why it was happening or what was happening to me. If you've been through this as an Autistic person, then you know how scary it can feel. If you know someone who is Autistic, know that this may happen to them and it will feel scary to them also.

Burnouts can also happen on a small or large scale, which is what I refer to as a daily burnout vs notable burnout. Both are completely valid burnout points, but the daily is more typical of what happens when needs are otherwise met outside of the current day. Notable burnouts are when needs are not met and cannot be met for an extended period of time, which leads to a longer recovery time as well. A daily burnout for me can take anywhere from one to three days to recover from, but a notable burnout can take years.

Meltdowns can also be scary and are not controllable. A meltdown can look like a lot of things, especially to the outside person, but what it actually is the inability to adapt or cope with a situation. In younger people, this could look like a tantrum. In adults, this could look like a controllable, intentional thing. The most important thing to remember is that a meltdown is actually none of those things. During a meltdown, I feel out of control of everything — the situation at hand, my ability to cope and adjust to it, as well as my ability to control my reactions. After a meltdown, I feel embarrassed and fatigued. They can be both a mental and physical thing, and many times I end up physically tired or sore. Sometimes, the ability to speak or use words is lost. When I'm nearing a meltdown or a daily burnout, using words begins to almost become a painful process — first speaking them, then as the feeling intensifies, even writing them. Having soothing things to help prevent this point from happening is crucial. Those are usually the times when I most enjoy watching a favorite repeat TV show or movie that I like. Consistency and reliability are at the root of most of my comforts.

Self-stimulating behaviors, also called "stimming," are very helpful for us Autistics to soothe. This a vague category box that contains an infinite list of personal stims unique to each person. While we can share similar stimming behaviors, the intensity or effect we're craving or receiving from it varies. I've never been one to enjoy peripheral equipment or toys, but I still enjoy the sensations — example: I don't much enjoy using tangle hand toys, but I do like flicking my fingers hard or feeling my nail surface. Dancing, face touching, rocking/swaying, these are also favorites for me. I have been spending a lot of time unlearning personal restriction around this after being taught or observing that it wasn't okay to do in front of others. Suppressing these soothing stimulations does not do anything positive for anyone; it only further grounds feelings of existential angst and an inability to survive day-to-day in the world. For the argument of "why can't you just not do it?" I would argue back, "why can't you just let someone take care of themselves?" There is an unhealthy generalized stigma around what types of self-care or medication is socially acceptable, but the real answer is that any type that impacts you positively is just that: a positive.

Whether or not you know you're Autistic, if you are, you'll probably be no stranger to pressure — pressure to adapt to things that don't feel natural, pressure to pretend that you don't need things, pressure to be less like yourself and more like "everyone else." I don't give in to peer pressure or small-scale social pressure easily because I am firm in my beliefs and values, but it is hard to resist the pressure from an entire societal view. That is where masking comes in for many Autistics as we try to blend in and look less out of place. But masking has a cost, and that cost can become losing ourselves. We become increasingly distraught over time at trying to meet demands we can't meet while feeling constant internal conflict at what we know we need, vs what we are allowing ourselves. We do not become less Autistic doing this because that is not a part of us that can be lost or removed. Eventually, either we must learn how to unmask, or we risk hitting burnout from the constant drain.

Not every Autistic has the ability or safety to unmask, which also means not every Autistic has the ability or safety to fully thrive at their true potential. Awareness is a good voice, but without acceptance in conjunction, its message echoes against a closed door. I have recently begun advocating on social media for Autism acceptance in hopes to destroy harmful stigmas and inaccurate stereotypes. Already, it has been one of the most meaningful and rewarding projects I have taken on, and I have found a sense of belonging within the Autistic community that is unlike any other connection I've known. It is also a lot of work, and I have to be mindful to recharge often. If you know any advocates, take a minute to thank them for their efforts!

My experiences in life have been unique to both myself as well as my neurological wiring, and I recognize that. Living a life of misunderstanding and intensity has also lent me the ability to try to see the good in people and to innately understand that everyone comes from different situations and backgrounds and shouldn't be judged, positively or negatively, by what we can see on the outside. My clothing is rarely appropriate for the occasion or weather, I find it very unnatural feeling to smile, and making prolonged eye contact feels about as comfortable as standing in a spotlight naked. As someone who has always been "that person" to someone else, I really understand what it's like to be misunderstood.

One last thing I want to share, but possibly the most important thing I hope everyone remembers — because it is relatable to so many Autistics I've spoken with is that while communication may be difficult for me, I still crave connection. I'm not always able to speak,] and I'm not always able to write, but I never want to feel alone. I seek time away from others in order to recharge, to be by myself, but it is not to be isolated or feel lonely. Sometimes, it is easier to remove myself from a situation rather than try to push through it because I know the cost it will take on me. Advocating for yourself and your needs can be difficult to learn, especially when you have to unlearn a life of quieting yourself in order to survive. If you know an]Autistic person who says they need something, listen to them, and please remember that the ability to use verbal words is not synonymous with the ability to communicate, just as neither are the inabilities of those. We can hear, we can see, we absorb.

I tend to think that being Autistic is quite great, but I also think there are environmental factors that can make it downright unbearable sometimes. I wouldn't want to change being Autistic, but I do wish the world was a little more empathetic towards differently wired needs.

Kevin Galbreth

My name is Kevin Galbreth. I am a 33 year old male with Asperger's disorder, a term that has recently been merged with Autism in the Diagnostic and Statistical Manual (DSM). This is my story of what it's like living with Autism. I would like to start off by thanking both Aidan Allman-Cooper and Jessica Leichtweisz for including me in their book, *This is Autism,* and giving me a chance to share my experiences of living with Autism. I would also like to thank both of my parents, (Cynthia Sergi and Edward Galbreth), for supporting me and advocating for me as well as they have over the years to make all of this possible.

Chapter 4: "Searching for Answers"

By Kevin Galbreth

My life experiences of living with Autism are a mixture of ups and downs as well as highs and lows. I suppose it's not much different from just about everyone. Overall, my life story is more of a success story than not, especially considering some of the problems I had when I was in elementary school. There is, however, still a lot of room for improvement and I still experience plenty of challenges that my Asperger's/Autism presents.

I will start off by giving some background information on me and an overview of my school life. When I first started my school life, I struggled with adapting. I was frequently in trouble for acting out in class and teasing peers. I struggled with learning how to appropriately interact with peers and would therefore often deliberately interact in inappropriate ways because I enjoyed the attention I would get for it. I was also constantly being disruptive in class, usually by making funny noises, and could rarely get through a full day without getting in trouble. I was evaluated and diagnosed with Asperger's in

December of 1993; right as Asperger's was being introduced to the DSM. I was in first grade at the time. My teachers wanted to either medicate me or place me in a self-contained classroom, both of which my parents were against. My parents believed I could be successful with the support of a one-to-one paraprofessional, so I ended up being in regular classrooms with the support of a paraprofessional from 1st-8th grade. While my behavior was still very challenging to deal with, I had excellent support from paraprofessionals who did an excellent job at keeping my behavior in check and really were invaluable with getting me through my grade school years. When I reached high school, I finally began to outgrow a lot of my behaviors and no longer needed the support of paraprofessionals. I also became much more focused academically in high school and began to excel with less extra support. College is my biggest success story of all. Without using any special supports and accommodations, I graduated Suny Cortland, summa cum laude, with a 4.12 GPA! My degree was in inclusive special education. This to this date is my proudest accomplishment. It unfortunately, however, wasn't really the fairy tale/Hollywood ending of me going on to continue to prosper like that throughout my adult life that I naively thought it would be at the time.

Having all the academic success in college somewhat blinded me to the challenges that awaited me after college when I stepped into the real adult world of making a good career for myself. I chose special education as my major due to wanting to use my personal experience of growing up with a disability to help others with disabilities overcome the obstacles of their disability and reach their full potential. While I excelled in the college classroom of writing papers and taking tests, I learned the hard way that that didn't necessarily translate to being good at working hands-on with children in a special education classroom. I very much struggled with student teaching at the very end of my college coursework. I just barely passed and definitely didn't feel like I was anywhere near ready to go and be a teacher. I also generally felt at that point that teaching didn't play to my strengths and it was time for me to think about a different career direction. Since then, I've been working as a direct support professional in residential homes for adults with developmental disabilities, making just a few dollars above minimum wage. My work there has mostly involved assisting adults with developmental disabilities with activities of daily living. While I've generally had some fulfilling experiences doing that kind of work, I feel somewhat underchallenged in it as it's a job that only requires a high school diploma and I've been doing it for seven years with a college degree. I've generally been at a crossroads since I left college and am struggling to figure out what is my best course of action for a good long term career path.

Now I will discuss some of the unique challenges as well as strengths that I feel is manifested in my Asperger's/Autism that are relevant to my life story and experiences. My biggest challenge today, I feel, comes in the area of self-confidence. The struggles I had in adapting socially growing up, as well as the self-awareness that I'm different and the fear that others will perceive my difference as negative has caused me to be way too concerned and even paranoid about what others think of me. I am constantly worried about others judging me in a negative way so I tend to be very shy about taking social risks. For example, I have never been in a romantic relationship. This is largely because I am too shy about approaching women I like and asking them out on dates out of fear of being turned down. You can say that I'm yet to grow out of the awkward and shy stage of adolescence. I will also tend to avoid social situations in which I don't know many people and only stick to going to social events in which there are people I know well and am comfortable with. My low confidence in social situations also often leads to me being non-confrontational to a fault. I tend to be overly concerned about upsetting others and will therefore be vulnerable to being a people pleaser that others may take advantage of. I have slowly but surely been learning to draw the line over the years, however, and am definitely improving with advocating for myself. I am also happy to say that I've been very fortunate to have an excellent group of close friends throughout my life. I tend to rely heavily on others initiating with me in social situations and once I get to know someone and am comfortable with them, I will be good with opening up more to them. I've been fortunate enough to have always had a great group of friends throughout my life who took that initiative with me. I am also really content with having a small group of really close friends and don't feel I need the large quantity. I believe in quality over quantity and all I need is a few high quality friendships. I am generally more of a loner and never see myself being a major social butterfly. The only thing I feel I've really been missing socially is a romantic relationship. A big part of me wants the experience of a romantic relationship, but there is also a part of me who doesn't take that lightly given the complications it brings.

I think my low self-confidence also holds me back with advancing vocationally. While I understand that the jobs I've been in are low-paying and dead end, I am also very comfortable and familiar with the work. I tend to be very shy about leaving my comfort zone and trying new things out of fear of failure. My fear of how others judge me in social situations also manifests in fear of how others will judge if I mess up with something and appear incompetent. I therefore tend to avoid attempting anything that I am unsure of my abilities in, out of not wanting to be judged negatively if I don't look like I know what I'm doing. Deep down, however, I know I am probably capable of way more than I think I am and should be less afraid of failing. I understand failing is often a rite of passage that we all have to go through to achieve our life goals. I also understand most people won't label me as incompetent for messing up one time, especially if I am new to something. It is generally said that you have to push yourself out of your comfort zone to advance in life. There's the old saying "nothing ventured, nothing gained." With all this being said, it is much easier said than done.

I will also admit that I tend to be very sensitive to criticism due to my fragile self-confidence. I often get defensive when someone is giving me constructive criticism out of worrying that it means they don't think I know what I'm doing. I may not always react out loud to being corrected, but internally, I may be thinking a bunch of paranoid thoughts about appearing incompetent.

I think all of this fragile self-confidence may be rooted in me wanting to camouflage my disability. Although I am well aware that I have a disability, I don't want it to be obvious to people around me. I am therefore overly concerned with appearing competent in all situations and tend to avoid situations I am less comfortable with in which my disability may be exposed more.

My low self-confidence is definitely my biggest challenge. I will now talk about some unique strengths I have that I successfully utilized in the past and hope to one day utilize again to get to where I want to be in life. My biggest unique strength is probably my long term memory. I remember just about every year of my life starting from when I was about six or seven and could write a detailed summary of what I did from then until now. If someone were to ask me what I was doing on a certain date years ago, there's a good chance I'd be able to remember and vice versa, there's a good chance I'd be able to name the date and year in which a memorable event happened. I also tend to remember things long term that are of particular interest to me. For example, as an avid sports fan, I can say who played in the championship round every year going back to when I first started following the sport and who won. The NFL is by far the sport I'm the biggest fan of and am unfortunately a long suffering fan of the New York Jets. Going back to when I first started following the Jets in 1997, I can name in order which teams they played and whether they won or lost. There are many games that I can even remember the score of.

I also have very good analytical skills, especially pertaining to areas of interest. I can go into a deep detailed analysis in talking or writing about topics I have an interest and am knowledgeable in. This, combined with my memory skills, really helped me do as well as I did in college. I was able to channel my memory skills to recall the details of what I would read in a textbook or hear in a classroom lecture/discussion. I would then write a very good paper filled with in-depth and insightful detailed analysis.

One other area of strength for me is my discipline, focus, and responsibility. It is often said that people with Autism or Asperger's tend to be avid with following rules. I'd say this is definitely true for me. I did as well as I did in college largely because I focused hard on my studies and didn't allow myself to get distracted by the wild party scene that a lot of college students do. Throughout my work life so far, I've been a very reliable and responsible employee. I am almost always on time for my shifts and on rare occasions when I'm not, there are extenuating circumstances. I always come ready to work and make doing my job my number one priority while I'm on duty. I look to put my best foot forward every day in the workplace and am not one to pick days to slack off.

I talked in the above paragraphs about how being risk averse is one of my weaknesses. I also, however, think it is a strength for me in certain areas. I am definitely not a reckless person who will go out and do dangerous things that many people get themselves killed doing. Erring on the side of caution has especially helped me become a very good driver. I am happy to say that I have maintained a clean driving record through 14 years of being a licensed driver. I think this is largely because I'm not one to do a lot of the reckless things that some drivers do like drinking and driving or totally disregarding traffic laws. I stick to a safe speed and obey the rules of the road.

I think driving is definitely one other area of success in my life. When I first reached the driving age, a lot of people were probably rightfully concerned about me learning to drive. This was largely due to my tendency to space out and daydream a lot when driving is a task that requires 100% focus and attention at all times. My reaction times and reflexes are a bit slower as well. While it took me a little longer than average to learn the basics of driving, I still nonetheless became a fine driver. I've been disciplined enough to not daydream while driving and compensate for my slower reflexes by maintaining a safe speed and following distance. The only thing I struggle with today is parking in narrow spaces, but I can often compensate for that by parking farther away and I have no trouble on the roads. I've been regularly driving on the expressways of New Jersey, (one of the toughest states to drive in), for several years now and have even driven some 16 passenger vans with my job. This is something I am definitely proud of as I know driving doesn't come easy to some people with Autism. I think driving is one of the few areas in which I have good self-confidence in.

As you can see, there is a combination of things I feel good and not so good about where I am at in life. I am happy to have prospered in certain areas that are often challenging for individuals with Autism. I also feel, however, that I have a lot of unfinished business with regards to achieving my life's goals, most especially in the area of career development/advancement. While I am happy to have held down a job providing a valuable service to the disabled community for as long as I have, I feel there are more advanced things out there that I am very much capable of doing. I especially look up to famous people with Autism like Temple Grandin and Alex Plank who learned how to use their unique abilities to make really great careers for themselves. I think Autism can really be as much of a gift as it is a disability if an individual with Autism properly utilizes his or her unique abilities. I really hope to one day find my niche in a good career field that best utilizes my strengths. I think one of the biggest keys for me to achieving this will be for me to let go of my fear of failure as well as how others may judge me and go out and try new things.

SUSAN ABRAMOWSKI

Sue Abramowski is an Autistic self-advocate who has 16 years of experience working with others who have developmental disabilities and mental illness. She earned her Bachelor's in Social Work from Buffalo State College in 2006. When she is not working one of her three jobs, Sue can be found tinkering with her Android devices, playing

Sonic the Hedgehog, or just chilling with her friends or family. Sue has a passion for helping others, and has been a people person for all of her 37 years!

Chapter 5: "Always a bit Different"

By Susan Abramowski

From the beginning, I've always been a bit "different." My story starts when I was in preschool. I was a spunky little thing who was very headstrong and marched to the beat of a different drummer. Here goes!

I remember it not occurring to me that I actually needed to DO what my teacher asked of me. I acted on a whim; if I wanted to go to the reading area and do cartwheels while the rest of my class was following a lesson, I did just that. There was one instance where I sat in the plastic Little Tikes playhouse, having a conversation with a beam of light casting on it. I was the poster child for ADHD. My teacher expressed concern and reached out to my parents. It was time for them to talk to a professional.

One day not long after this, my parents took me to an office where I climbed up a few flights of stairs. I remember then sitting in a room where I played with toys as my parents talked to a psychologist. What they talked about I really wasn't paying attention to, as I was busy focusing on a never-ending yo-yo of a sort which circled around a wire track.

I probably should have been diagnosed with SOMETHING at this point, namely ADHD, however from what my parents have told me, the psychologist's wife had a baby, and he never touched base with them afterwards, all before I had a chance to complete any kind of screening. Thus, I flew under the radar, which would go on for the next several years of my life.

Next came elementary school. Kindergarten. I recall going to the school for my pre-Kindergarten screening. There was a lady who asked me to do various tasks and I completed each. I still remember the pink windbreaker jacket I was wearing. My mom mentioned years later that the lady had mentioned something about my gross motor skills. To this day, I'm a klutz!

I still struggled to follow directions. My teacher would often write, "Susan does what Susan wants to do" on my report card. I hadn't lost that impulsivity. I was my own leader. I managed to do well in class, regardless.

In first grade, something finally clicked, to the point

where it finally dawned on me that my teacher was telling me what I needed to do for a REASON and that I was to do it! I wanted to be a "good" kid and do what I was told. My teacher told my parents I was a great student and excelled in reading. My mom had asked her if my behavior had ever been a problem and my teacher had told her that it hadn't at all and that I was well-behaved. Who'd have thought?

My second grade teacher embraced me for the unique individual I was. She told my parents that she appreciated the fact I was different from the other kids. She was an amazing teacher! She truly encouraged me to follow my heart and use my artistic talents.

The rest of elementary school went well and I earned high grades. At the same time, there was still a sort of disconnect between myself and the other kids. They would play and laugh together and I'd try to laugh along and get weird stares. As much of a social butterfly as I've always been, I still missed cues and nuances. I've always taken things very literally and at face value. I don't "read between the lines." I also had interesting quirks, like asking everyone in passing their shoe size when I was 9. I also began to experience the intrusive thoughts of OCD.

I met my best friend around this age. I remember she sat at the table adjacent to me in lunch. We would often chat and eventually became fast pals! She recalls a time, (and I hadn't remembered this), where she had told me another kid who sat at her table was weird and I had replied, "it's okay to be weird." I'm glad to know I saw nothing wrong with being different so early on. She ended up moving schools and I ran into her while at the library with my aunt about a year later, and then we didn't see each other for several years.

Middle school was where my differences really started becoming apparent. I had been obsessed with Sonic the Hedgehog since I first played the game at 9 and others teased me for this. It didn't faze me one way or another and I kept on being the die-hard *Sonic* fan I was. I also didn't go through a typical adolescence; when the other girls were suddenly preoccupied with things like boys and their appearance, I couldn't wrap my head around it. Those things just didn't matter to me, nor did the opinions of others. I was just me. The fact that my friends were changing and interested in different things seemingly overnight triggered my OCD further. Were they going to lose interest in hanging out with me? Were they still going to be the same? Would they leave me in the dust? These thoughts led to my asking a million and one reassurance questions and I probably drove them up a wall in the process. I would continue to do the same in high school.

I don't think I had a particularly out-of-the-ordinary high school experience as far as academics went. I continued to be a diligent and conscientious student and wanted to do the best I could. I had my subjects I mastered and others I had to work a little harder on. One thing I had noticed about myself from the get go, however, was that it was difficult to follow directions and stay on task. I was forgetful and would often mix things up or copy down homework assignments incorrectly, especially math problems. I had learned of ADHD when I was around 12 and a light bulb went off in my head immediately. It described me to a T! Any time I would tell my parents about it, they would brush it off, stating there was nothing "wrong" with me. I held onto my suspicions for several years.

One afternoon when I was in eleventh grade, I was in the locker room after gym along with another girl. We struck up a conversation. Over the course of the next few days, we would pass each other in the halls and talk some more. She then realized she remembered me from elementary school— I was the girl she had befriended at lunch! I was so glad to be reunited as I had wondered how she was doing for the past several years. This started what would become one of my longest and closest friendships! My best friend was in a self-contained classroom in the special education program, which meant she was in the same classroom for most of the day and was mainstreamed for lunch, gym, study hall, and an elective. We lucked out and ended up in lunch and study hall together! We shared many good times throughout the remainder of high school!

I had started working at McDonald's in my senior year of high school and held this job for a total of four years. I was a hard worker and wanted to be someone my coworkers could count on. My differences were apparent here, too; there were moments I stuck out like a sore thumb. I still wasn't interested in boys or dating and others seemed to think that was the strangest thing they'd ever encountered. I didn't see the big deal. I simply didn't have any desire to be in a relationship like many of them. I also didn't understand nor care for a lot of the suggestive topics they'd joke about. Things of that nature grossed me out.

I began college as a biology education major right after high school as I had loved the subject and felt it was my niche to teach it. Between school and work, I managed my schedule and workload, and again, did really well in some courses and had to work really hard in others. Three years into it, I realized that being a teacher didn't feel like my niche, after all. What I really wanted to do was help others. My best friend had moved to a group home shortly after high school and after hanging out with her regularly at her house, I met her staff and became familiar with what life at a group home was like: what the staff's duties were, the outings they went on, passing medications and such. I had also been her listening ear whenever she needed someone to talk to and I tried to give the best advice I could and be there for her. I felt driven to continue to work with people, which I found to be my true passion! I changed my major to social work and it was the best decision I could have made! I left fast food and began working in a group home with people who have developmental disabilities.

I graduated with my bachelor's in 2006. I lucked out and was offered two jobs on the same day about a month later! I accepted a full-time position working with people who have mental illness in a group home setting, as well as relief at another group home again with people who have developmental disabilities. I had still held a part-time position at a supervised apartment where I became employed after working in my first group home and went to relief status there once I had acquired the full-time position. I found myself with three jobs at once!

Surprisingly as hectic as it sounds, having three jobs was pretty manageable for me. While I've always been one to be easily overwhelmed while trying to carry several different plates, the concept of carrying ONE fully-loaded plate was something I could tackle! Executive functioning deficits bring with them difficulty multitasking. I can focus on one thing at a time and pour all of my energy into it, but the minute I try to add something else, I lose sight of something and all my energy goes to another single task.

The fact that I was mainly focusing on work with few outside responsibilities made it so that I could handle it all!

When I had been out of college for two years and was still working at the mental health group home, I did notice that I had some struggles. I would forget menial tasks here and there and forgetting to sign my timecard was something I was no stranger to. I finally decided to take the bull by the horns and investigate WHY I had the difficulties I had had my whole life. I sought out a psychologist and made an appointment for an ADHD assessment. It turns out that I had hit the nail on the head after all as it was confirmed! I was also diagnosed with OCD and anxiety around the same time.

It didn't even occur to me that I was Autistic until about a year later. I had always enjoyed reading articles by people with disabilities and mental illness as I love learning about personal experiences. One day, I stumbled upon a blog written by a girl around my age who was on the spectrum, and I felt like I was reading my life story. Much research ensued after that. I put two and two together and came to the conclusion that Autism just described much of what I had experienced over the course of my life. I wished to somehow be assessed, however I was under the misconception that it would cost me thousands of dollars, so I simply self-identified as autistic. Once again, my parents were a little skeptical of my conclusion at first, but the more I talked with them, the more they began to understand.

I had linked with a new psychiatrist about five years later and after sharing my thoughts with her and expressing my interest in seeking an assessment, she suggested I go back to the psychologist who had diagnosed me with ADHD for an Autism assessment. Why hadn't I thought of that? I eagerly contacted his office and set up an appointment. The quest was on!

After the assessment process was complete and questionnaires were completed by my parents and I, it was time for the moment I was waiting for: I would finally get my answer! I guess I must really be good at figuring myself out because I did it yet again! On March 19th, 2014, my psychologist gave me a diagnosis of Autism Spectrum Disorder Level I! I was elated. I had such a sense of validation. I walked out of the office beaming.

This was a major turning point for me. It didn't change who I was; I was still the same Sue: *Sonic* fan, gamer, Android geek, and animal lover, but I now knew myself even better! There was a reason for the way some facets of me were the way they were after all. I have always been content with who I am and have never wanted to change for anyone, but this gave everything MEANING.

I had been active in the Autistic community on Facebook for the past five years and was familiar with self advocacy from both my best friend, who has been by my side all along the way, and some of the residents with whom I worked being involved in it. I had gone to several meetings. I joined a social group for Autistics at a local agency with whom I would eventually get a position after becoming impressed with the organization and seeking employment there. I met others in my shoes and fit right in. The executive director and I became very close and she offered me speaking engagements where I talked about my experience as an Autistic. Once I became an employee in their after school program, I felt valued as both a self advocate and member of the team! I continue to pick up respite and relief there, as I still continue to hold three jobs!

Currently, my full-time role is that of a behavioral management coordinator. I absolutely love it! I've always been very analytical and have wanted to know WHY people do the things they do. I enjoy coming up with solutions to maladaptive behaviors and most importantly of all, helping them to have the best quality of life they can! My third job is a relief position in another mental health group home. I care a lot for all the people with whom I work: my "peeps," as I call them.

I find it so interesting that it wasn't until after I began working in the field that I learned I was also a member of the developmental disabilities and mental health communities! I entered it wanting to help others around me and in turn, I learned a great deal about myself to boot. Everything happens for a reason and my path is just proof of this fact! Now I can take my experiences and use them to connect with others and establish a rapport with them. It was no coincidence that I've always connected with people who have disabilities; I've had a lot of the same experiences as they have because I am a member of the same community they are! Today, I grab hold of any opportunity I can to tell my story and to advocate for others. Thank you for reading!

Michelle Vinokurov

Born in Brooklyn, NY, Michelle was diagnosed with Autism at the young age of two. Despite some of the challenges she experienced in her earlier years such as eye contact, temper tantrums, and communication issues, Michelle is an absolute force to be reckoned with and has proven time and time again that despite the difficulties she may experience, her life is limitless. Currently, Michelle is a popular Keynote speaker and has had the opportunity to speak about what life is like living with Autism and also works as an instructional paraprofessional at a public school in New Jersey. In her free time, Michelle creates posts and entries on her inspiring blog, "The World of Autism," and regularly interviews and features guests on her blog to discuss issues and feelings that surround the Autism community.

Chapter 6: "Reaching Milestones"

By Michele Vinokurov

I was born on January 18, 1998 in Brooklyn, New York. During my first year, my parents said there were no noticeable issues until I reached the age when people normally begin to speak. They noticed by then that I was not responding when my name was called and any noises that were around us. My parents decided to seek out advice from doctors, in which they were comparing my developmental milestones to my older sister, Samantha. We went through the whole process to eliminate any other possible issues I may have had. One of the tests was for hearing loss to rule out any hearing issues. The audiologist said I was fine and ruled out hearing loss. After going through several tests, the results from all of the tests came out negative. Eventually, my parents and I were referred to a neurologist in Down State Hospital in Brooklyn, New York. This was when I officially was diagnosed with Autism in January of 2000; I was almost two years old at that time.

While living in Brooklyn, New York, my Autism affected me in many ways: I had no eye contact, I did not respond to anything, and I was completely nonverbal. I did not like anyone to touch me and I did not like anyone picking me up. I had temper tantrums and meltdowns. I used to spin as my stimming and I liked everything in a routine. I was isolated from my siblings: my older sister, Samantha, and my younger brother, Jon. I did not engage with anyone really; I was pretty much in my own world. I attended Thursday Child, a specialized school for individuals living with Autism—they provide Early Intervention services at school and at home. I attended school Monday through Friday for four hours per day and I received ABA Early Intervention services seven days a week at home. I will be honest and say that I do not recall much about myself during my early years living in New York.

When I was three years old in August of 2001, my family and I moved to Marlboro, New Jersey. We moved because my family grew in size and there weren't many services left for me in New York. My parents looked for a good school for me as soon as we moved to Marlboro. After my parents visited some schools such as Children's

Center of Monmouth County and Douglass Developmental Disabilities Center at Rutgers University, they decided with Children's Center of Monmouth County because they thought it was a better fit for me in terms of my supports and needs. Children's Center was a specialized school in Neptune, New Jersey for kids with Autism and multiple disorders. I was in a secluded classroom with students living with Autism like me and the school did not provide educational studies—it taught life skills. In my classroom, I was the only girl and the rest were boys. In school, I continued with the therapies that I received since very young. My pediatrician recommended that I see a neurologist to help with some behavioral issues I was having. My parents took me to see Dr. Sultan who confirmed my Autism diagnoses and made recommendations on treatments for my Autism. Dr. Sultan has been an instrumental part of my development and has treated several health issues I have had to deal with throughout my life. I am very grateful for his continuous care.

By the time I was 6 years old, I finally said my first word! I was slowly gaining to verbally communicate from there on. My only memory of Children's Center is the

Hawaiian dance I did with my second grade teacher, Mrs. Lauren, because we practiced it so much that I still remember that day. It was fun dancing with her! Eventually, my parents found out from the child study team in Children's Center that I was more advanced than most of my classmates. They said I was verbally communicating more and my behavior improved. My parents were advised that I was ready to be put back into the Marlboro Township School District. My parents were not convinced that I was ready, but I knew I was ready for more.

I actually remember when I went to visit my future public school in June of 2006. I went inside of the school building with my dad and we met with the principal and one of the teacher assistants, Mrs. Russo. In the classroom, I remember meeting my future teacher, Mrs. DeWynGeart, (Mrs. Hemschoot). I was sitting at a desk with my name tag on it and a blue notebook with my name on it. I was shy around the other students, but I was smiling about being in the class. My first real public school I attended was Frank Dugan Elementary School.

In September 2006, I attended Frank Dugan Elementary School. I came into Marlboro Township School

District as a new student and I was still taking a minivan bus as my transportation to school. Attending Dugan entailed new challenges for me. I remember being scared about my first day in a new school. I was very shy and I did not know how to make friends, even though I wanted to. I was fortunate that a couple of classmates came up to me and they became my first friends in that school: George and Gabby D. The three of us were together a lot, from lunch to recess to class. The three of us always had a fun time together. Today, they are still good friends to me and I still keep in touch with them.

While in Dugan, I was in a special education self-contained classroom filled with less than 15 students, including me. I was in that classroom for math and reading since I didn't receive educational studies before, although I was placed in a general education classroom for social studies and science. It was very different for me being in a classroom that had a lot more students, but I was provided with a teacher assistant in the classroom. I was pulled-out for one-to-one classroom assistance for that class. During my one-to-one sessions, my teacher assistant went over any topics that needed clarification as well as reviewed and prepared me for any upcoming exams. In math, I was allowed to use the number line system to assist me when working on math problems. Another one of my accommodations was for me to sit in the front of the classroom, which I did all of my school years. I received a number of therapies by the Child Study Team in Dugan: physical, speech, and occupational therapy. I still remember when I first learned to hold a pencil because it reminds me of when I began to learn to write. That was a big milestone for me and I am very proud of that. I believe that being in a public school surrounded by supportive teachers and students really helped me achieve many of my goals.

My parents learned at an IEP meeting that I was also eligible for extended school year. Since there were no appropriate summer school accommodations for me in the school district, the Child Study Team from Dugan and the special services administration allowed me to attend a camp for special needs children over the summer. They recommended a camp in my town called "Harbor Haven". The camp was only ten minutes away from my house. I liked the camp so much that I ended up going there for four summers. I recall the field trips I went on every Friday—playing in the inflatables every other week, swimming in the large pool, learning to cook, playing on the computers, having music time, playing various kinds of sports, and learning karate and yoga. Best of all, being with an amazing group of camp friends. My camp friends were: Gabby, Daniella, Jenny, and Ashlee. After camp, I lost contact with everyone. After many years later, I am so happy to share that I was able to reconnect with Gabby and Daniella. I did not even know if they still would remember me or not, but they both still do. The three of us reunited for my twenty first birthday since I invited them and all of my best friends together to celebrate. In all, Harbor Haven was the best choice for me to attend camp. I made so many experiences with camp that I will never forget, including the friendships that were created.

When I was going into 4th grade, I was transferred to Robertsville Elementary School. I still had the same teacher and all the same services, but our class had to move due to space issues in Frank Dugan Elementary School. It was definitely a challenge for me adjusting to a new school again, but I got through it from the support of my family and teachers. I stopped having physical and occupational therapy in 4th grade. I improved so much that I only needed speech therapy. I knew I was improving myself because I was getting better pronouncing words more clearly during speech therapy. Furthermore, I signed up for band in fourth grade because I remember my older sister's band concerts and it looked so much fun getting to play an instrument. I ended up loving band so much myself that I did it again in fifth grade. I enjoyed band a lot because I got to learn to play an instrument. I played the clarinet. Two things came into my mind at that time: I grew up watching *SpongeBob SquarePants*, so I wanted to play the clarinet better than Squidward. I thought the clarinet was an interesting and easy instrument to play. I was always so happy and proud about how well I played with the clarinet and the band concerts were so much fun! My experiences with band was the beginning of me performing in front of an audience.

After graduating from Robertsville Elementary School, I attended Marlboro Middle School. It was the first school I ever attended with my siblings. I was so happy now to attend the same school with my siblings. It did not bother me much about being in a different school than my siblings, but it was exciting to now be with them in school too. I finally started taking the big bus with the other neighborhood kids in my community.

Middle school was a big adjustment for me. Starting in sixth grade, I struggled with using a locker. I had difficulty opening my locker since it was a combination lock. I used to get so frustrated about it! I told my parents about that, we talked to the Child Study Team, and accommodations were made for me to use a key to open my locker. I used a key for my locker throughout all of my middle school years. It made me feel better and less anxious. I want to let everyone know—do not be afraid to ask for accommodations for anything, even if it's for something as simple as a key for a locker.

Furthermore, I finally learned and understood about Autism in sixth grade. We were at a family friend's house one day and we watched Dr. Temple Grandin's HBO documentary film. After the film, my parents shared how I was like Dr. Temple in some ways. From there, I finally began to understand how I live differently from everyone. I was shocked at first, but learning about living with Autism helped me learn about myself a lot, especially in many good ways.

I was showing so much improvement in school that my mom signed me up for taekwondo classes at ATA Black Belt Academy. My mom wanted me to learn self-defense because it would help me improve my motor skills and self-control. It turned out to be my favorite activity of all time! I will never forget my experience there! I was one of the couple of students with a disability that was put into regular taekwondo classes. It showed that I was able to perform like everyone else, even though I learn differently. Successfully, I earned my black belt when I was ten years old! It was December of 2008. My older sister, Samantha and I earned our black belts on the same day! It showed that having Autism did not stop me from earning my black belt. This was the beginning of learning self-confidence because I learned I can be successful and perform like everyone else.

Throughout middle school, I continued to receive modifications and accommodations like speech and teacher assistants in the classroom. In sixth grade, I was in all resource classrooms in every subject-content area: math, language arts, science, and social studies. In seventh grade, I moved up for the first time for math into a general education classroom with a teacher assistant. My teacher assistant was there to assist me if I needed any clarification; all I had to do was raise my hand. My teacher assistant was also available during lunch for any extra help I needed.

By eighth grade, I moved up to all general education classes, except for science. My parents continued to meet with the Child Study Team once a year to go over my progress and review my accommodations I may need. One of my modifications was to have extra time on tests and to have two choices instead of four on all multiple-choice tests. I was also allowed to have the test questions read aloud to me if needed. With my parents, I attended all of my individualized education plan meetings during my middle school years.

I will never forget my influential speech teacher, Mrs. Smith. At first, I was only with her for speech. In eighth grade, she created a class for all students with special needs within the school to help kids learn social skills. I attended my social skills class once a week. She created an amazing program that I learned various social skills topics, from making friends to facing with bullying. I improved tremendously with my social skills. I made my own group of friends at lunch in 8th grade and they are now and still my best friends today! My best friends are: Shelby, Alyssa, Hilary, Justina, Jenna, and Sam. I met them all throughout my middle school years through classes, but came altogether in lunch. The social skills class helped me apply what I have learned to generalize into my social environments and things became more natural for me from there.

Besides everything that went on in school, I learned I was going to be a big sister again when I was in seventh grade. In 2010, my mom was pregnant with my little sister, Ariella. When I learned Ariella was coming, I was so happy to become a big sister again and I was nervous too. I was worried that Ariella would not understand what it means to have an older sibling with Autism. Ariella came into the family in December 2010 and I love her so much. She is the most empathic, little sister.

Before graduating from middle school, I got to choose between attending Colts Neck High School and Marlboro High School. It was one of my biggest decisions I had to make; I was choosing either to be with the majority of my best friends or being with my older sister, Samantha.

After taking in all the pros and cons, I choose to attend Colts Neck High School after graduating middle school. I received a sibling waiver since Samantha was a student already attending the high school. I was excited for my high school years in Colts Neck High School, but I faced obstacles going into my freshman year.

I was finally mainstreaming in general education classrooms which had special education teachers co-teaching with general education teachers. I was struggling to keep up because it took me more time to take notes and process everything they were saying, as well as needing more time on exams. Sometimes, I did not get to finish taking my exams because they would not allow me to. It turned out that my high school had never received my individualized education plan files and they had no idea that I was classified with Autism. I was having anxiety over various issues in school, so I told my parents about the difficulty I was having. My parents called my guidance counselor to set up a meeting to discuss my disability and get my special education services. After meeting with the Child Study Team case manager/psychologist, Mr.Schaffer, all the issues were resolved and they started providing all the necessary special education services I needed. My first month of high school proved to me that my parents are always there to support me and make sure I get the resources I need to do well in school. I continued to receive services like speech therapy, support from my special education teacher teaching with a general education teacher, and longer test taking times. I always reached out to the teachers for assistance when I needed extra help. Being in regular school taught me how to advocate for things that I needed and taught me to reach out to my teachers and not be afraid to ask for help.

I had other challenges in my freshman year of high school, which include relationships with my peers. There was someone who I thought they were a friend to me since I knew them since middle school, but they went behind my back one day and even started to spread rumors about me. Everything that this person was saying about me was not true. Eventually, they were saying threatening words to me that was making me upset when I was coming home from school. I told my parents about this when it got to that point and they told me to go to my Child Study Team case manager/psychologist, Mr. Schaffer. I did do that and we talked together with this person who was being mean to me. The situation was resolved peacefully, but I learned from this to reach out for help. There are many people who will help and support you in situations like this one.

Despite these challenges in my freshman year, I began to learn the importance of volunteering with my siblings. This continued throughout the rest of my high school years. Back towards the end of eighth grade, my siblings and I became volunteers for my town's organization called "Marlboro TAC". Some things I volunteered for through this organization were: planting trees in Marlboro's REC Center, organizing and lining up students backstage for Frank Dugan Elementary School's yearly talent show, Marlboro Day, and Champions, a before and after care program in Marlboro Township School District. To this day, I learned the importance of helping others and giving back to the community. Plus, I learned more about my interests by being in extracurricular activities in my high school. I signed up for my first club in high school, American Sign Language Club. I started learning American Sign Language on my own because of my best friend, George, who could not hear in one ear. I loved American Sign Language, so I continued to learn and was a member of the high school's ASL club for the entire time I was in high school. From there, I continued to learn, practice, and use American Sign Language. I learned the importance of helping others through volunteering and exploring interests through extracurricular activities.

In my junior year of high school, after overcoming my personal issues and adjusting to mainstream classrooms, I decided to be a Peer Mentor to students with various disabilities in an after-school program called Cougar Connections. My older sister, Samantha, was a peer mentor because she was inspired by me to help others living with disabilities. That really meant a lot to me and this was when I started to find interest in helping individuals living with disabilities. We did activities like arts and crafts and attended school sports events. I wanted to not just be a mentor, but a friend too. Also, I became secretary of the Book club, and a member of the National Honor Society. As mentioned, I was still a member of the ASL club. I felt at this point I was learning what I am really into and it's important for people to find their own interests and passions.

Along the way, I made more relationships with peers in and out of school. I created a lot of acquaintances in my classes and lunch period. In gym class, I made my first group of friends in which not everyone was in the same grade as me. I called them my FAM friends: Joe, Justina, (my best friend since middle school), Ashley L, Sam, Nick F, and Kevin. In Book Club: Nick, Megan, and Natalie. In American Sign Language Club: Joyce, Katrina, Courtney, and Shawna. In Marlboro TAC, I became friends with Isabelle, who attended my high school but met her from volunteering when we planted trees at Marlboro REC center. Everyone I met has taught me about creating and maintaining good friendships by keeping in touch on social media and hangouts.

I will never forget my experience learning to drive. I passed my driver's education class during my sophomore year with no problem, acing the permit test on my first try. On the other hand, learning to drive was completely different for me. It took me a while practicing driving in the community before getting out of the community. I practiced merging, parallel parking, making turns, turning on red when making a right turn when safe to do so, judging when the road is clear to go on, and etc. I even practiced on the day of my surprise birthday party when my dad made me drive to get pizza in pouring rain and thunder. I took my road test a couple of days after my seventeenth birthday, passed my road test on the first try, and got my driver's license! I have been driving ever since.

In my senior year in high school, I chose to stop my speech therapy that I have been getting since I was very young. I knew I was doing better at this point in my life and I knew there would be no therapies after high school. I was proud to have made my own decision because it proved I was becoming independent in my decisions and being a self-advocate. Also, I was one of the sixty students in my high school to be a peer leader in the high school's peer leadership program. One of the experiences I will never forget as a peer leader was providing presents to children at Union Beach Elementary School, since they were affected by Hurricane Sandy.

In June of 2016, I graduated from Colts Neck High School with four principal honor rolls, getting straight A'), being in the National Honors Society, academic student of the month, and two awards from Senior Awards Night. Not only that, I gave my first keynote speech for the Dare to Dream Disability Leadership Conference as a keynote speaker! I got my first job as a teacher assistant for Champions, the before and after care program in Marlboro

Township School District I volunteered for! I still work this job today as my second job.

After Colts Neck High School, I decided to attend Brookdale Community College. There were a lot of reasons why I decided to attend there. My family, teachers, best friends, and my friend from high school, Ashley A, supported me in this decision to attend Brookdale. Ashley gave me a tour of the college as a tour guide since she was working on campus there and was already attending Brookdale. She was really informative about the college through her personal and professional experiences at Brookdale. I learned from her how Brookdale was the best fit for me. I am so thankful she helped me through that time!

As soon as I knew that I got into college, I went to disability services provided by Brookdale Community College. I registered through the disability services with the case manager, Ernest Oversen. I choose what modifications and accommodations meet my needs. My modifications and accommodations were listed on an Alert form. Every class that I took, I provided the professors with my Alert fom and we discussed my accommodations and modifications. My professors were very accommodating. I was fortunate to have had a lot of good professors. Brookdale Community College also offers students with special needs a vocational program called KACH. The students get job career experience and classroom experience at the college.

I started Brookdale right away after graduating from high school by taking a summer class. I had to take a remedial class since I did not do well in the placement exam. I am glad I did that because it kept me in pace of my goal, which was to finish in two to three years. I spread out my course load each semester and took classes online and in person. To balance with work, I worked part time; I worked three to four days a week and mainly just after care hours. This way, I had time to focus on my college work. I learned a lot about time management and balancing priorities between college work and my job.

Besides from everything I was doing, I ended up getting more keynote speaking opportunities from special education organizations and special education organization parent advisory groups in New Jersey, including in my town, Marlboro! I am thankful for the opportunities because

I enjoy providing families, educators, professionals, and therapists, valuable information about Autism.

While attending Brookdale, I got involved in the education club. I knew I was going for a career in the education field. From the support of my education-field professors, my family, and my friends, I became a co-president of the education club in my last year of college. As a co-president, these were some things I learned: being a leader in my own ways, collaboration, and communication with my co-president, secretary, and club advisors. I co-hosted club meetings and events, and even included speakers in the education field. In addition, I was featured on Brookdale Community College's social media platforms in their student success stories series, "The Souls of Brookdale." I spoke for the Governor's group of the college by sharing my success experiences at Brookdale.

Last May, I graduated from Brookdale Community College. I graduated from Brookdale Community College as a Distinguished Scholar with a 3.9 GPA, a member of the National Society of Leadership and Success and as co-president of the education Club. I earned my Associate's Degree of Applied Science.

Currently, I work as a paraprofessional in an elementary school working with students that have Autism. I continue to work my part time job as a teacher assistant for the Champions program in Marlboro as my second job. I love working with elementary school children! I am a committee member of the New Jersey Autism Think Tank. I have been fortunate to perform keynote speeches for special education organizations and special education parent advisory groups throughout New Jersey. I am a blogger of my own blog series website, "The World of Autism." I have been one of the main panelists for Mrs. Jessica Leichweitsz's, "Ask an Autistic" webinar series, as well as I was interviewed by her for her other series, "Bridge the Gap". I am different in my own ways, but I am not less different than everyone else.

RACHEL BARCELLONA

A graduate of Dunedin High School who successfully
completed her junior year at the University of South
Florida, double majoring in English and communications,
Rachel is an active advocate for those with disabilities. Part
of her advocacy was creating a non-profit, The Ability
Beyond Disabilities, to inspire and help those that have

challenges to strive for their dreams as well as to educate those who might not understand the challenges faced.

As an individual with Autism and epilepsy, Rachel was targeted by bullying and harassment, as well as countless individuals with disabilities or anyone with differences. Despite the challenges that she has faced, Rachel credits her life and social experience in allowing her to overcome such obstacles. Today, Rachel is a spokesperson for the Center for Autism and Related Disabilities at the University of South Florida (CARD-USF) and is also on their board. She also holds board positions at Unicorn Children's Foundation, The Els Center for Excellence as well as the Dyspraxia Foundation USA, all of which provide services to individuals with disabilities including occupational, physical, music, and art therapy. As people with Autism are reaching ages of employment, her primary focus now has been to bring awareness to individuals and companies that are offering employment opportunities for Autistic individuals.

Rachel has won many state and national pageant titles and has performed the national anthem at major sports events, as well as performing at Madison Square Garden. She also spoke at the United Nations on World Autism Day and recently filmed a short documentary for Sephora. Currently, Rachel works at a radio station in New York and has her own segment. Additionally, Rachel is an avid writer and is currently working on developing a series of fantasy novels.

Chapter 7: "Journey to the Crown: Stimming and Finally Winning"

By Rachel Barcelona

I can distinctly remember being diagnosed with Autism at the age of three, my mom, who to this day wears a smile on her face, bright and happy-looking clothes and overly hairsprayed blonde hair that came straight out of the eighties sat with me in the Principal's office of my very conservative Christian preschool with confused eyes, wondering why she was pulled from yet another day of work to come and help me out.

I didn't understand why I didn't like to play with the other kids at school, it was so overwhelming, and I couldn't stand it. The noise during playtime was like an icepick to my ears, I often hid in the bathroom for hours just so I could avoid it all. It was okay for me, everyone though I was weird anyway. However, the teachers finally thought that they had enough of my behavior and sent me to the almighty ruler of the office with my mom waiting for me, almost knowing what they would say. I wasn't prepared for doctors to surround the principal in that office like they were running tests or something; there was something definitely wrong here, and I was in trouble.

"Your daughter has Autism," principal lady said, adjusting her glasses. "We ran some tests, and that's the reason why she's not playing with the other kids; she won't even look them in the eye."

"So what?" My mom tried really hard not to cry. "She's still a person."

"She'll never have any friends with the way she behaves," one doctor chimed in. "The teachers have described her as almost antisocial, especially when a song comes on."

He embarrassingly referred to all the times we had to get up and dance to those stupid kids songs, they were loud and I really hated them, especially since I was used to the likes of classical music to my dad's various albums from the seventies that I listened to for music therapy. This was a weird social event that kids loved for some reason, but I had no issue with sitting out. My mom became even more irate, hating what the doctors were saying about me. Antisocial, no friends, can't go to a real school, will never have a real job; all of this was nonsense.

"I'll be damned if my daughter has no friends!"

After some more talk with the principal regarding what to do with me and whatever, Mom and I walked out of the office. I asked her what Autism was, but she seemed a lot calmer now.

"It's just a difference, you're still a person." It was at that moment my mom never stopped her journey to help me be the person I am today.

***

My journey with Autism was very difficult, just like many people who are born with this disorder. It doesn't look like anything bad happened to me in life and if you look at me while walking on the street, you would probably think, "She has life all figured out; she's accomplished so much already, how could she be feeling sad or lonely?"

"How could she have Autism?"

That has been people's mantra that has graced my life for the better part of my adulthood and it's very easy for people to think that way. Life has been hard, but I worked very hard. I've gone on to show people that Autism isn't something to be ashamed of for at least eleven years, which led me to not only win crowns at pageants but earn leadership roles in my community of Autism acceptance, which means so much to me. But it didn't start out that way.

Autism is a spectrum; we are all different and progress at different rates. Many people compliment me on my exquisite vocabulary and how I am so articulate for my age, but before I was diagnosed, I barely knew how to talk. I can remember only saying a few distinct words. Time went on and while other kids were progressing in their vocabulary, I could only stay focused on the words that were written on the back of medicine bottles and a few lines from movies—my Kindergarten teachers became very concerned when I couldn't stop quoting from those late movie nights with my dad. That was awkward, but I tried my best.

***

Autism doesn't discriminate—it doesn't care about what you look like, your background, or what you will go through in life, which is what happened to me as I grew up. Kindergarten was vastly different, the loud noises surrounding the room and children screaming with joy assaulted my ears yet again. The only way I could calm myself down was something I knew very well. I rocked back and forth, often in a chair or standing up, an act I still do today when stressed; a lot of people don't even notice it. Stimming is an act that is commonly used by Autistic people when they're in stressful situations and it comes in many forms. We find our perfect stim and we feel calm doing it, whether it be rocking, flapping, singing, anything. Unfortunately, there's always that one person who has to say something about it.

"Who's that weird girl, she won't stop moving around!"

It was so embarrassing to go to the first day of school with so many kids crowding in one room and everyone noticing I was different already. I hid behind my teacher and stimmed again, this time feeling her dress, finding the fabric comforting. I felt attacked and I knew everyone was looking at me for a good reason. I was the weird one because I hated wearing those awful dresses all the girls wore, not only to their first day, but every day. They touched my skin, constricted me and my freedom; it was a sensory nightmare. The war on dresses was real as I tried really hard not to rip mine apart, hating the fabric and feeling itchy. I found the perfect stim again, rocking back and forth on my feet, flapping a little as some boys laughed at the state of me.

"Hey everybody, it's flappy!" One chanted as the class laughed. This day was going well.

***

Kindergarten was an endless game of throwing me around like a ragdoll, my teacher and other faculty members running around like frantic chickens trying to figure out what to do with me. I was confused when I got sent to other classes just for stimming—my teacher saying that I was causing a disturbance. It was really stupid, but I got used to it; ignorance became part of my life. In the middle of the year, things became different when my teacher finally decided enough was enough, causing my mom to be involved again. We were sitting in another principal's office, an all too familiar setting for me at this point. There were no doctors this time, but my teacher was there with a forceful message—ignorance had come to hit us like that one dodgeball in gym class that gave you a black eye; a hit that some could only describe as legendary but extraordinarily painful.

"We think your daughter would be better off in the retarded class," she said. "She would be less of a distraction and she'd be with others like her." The principal's eyes widened.

"Now," she said. "Let's not say things like that." My mom was visibly angry, but the teacher kept running her mouth, angry with me.

"What are you talking about!" She directed her brown eyes, full of hate at me. "She can't sit still and makes the other kids uncomfortable, what do you expect me to do?"

Mom couldn't stand it anymore, she was always great at letting her opinions be known and I had to deal with it. She stood from her chair and got in the teacher's face, not afraid of her one bit. My teacher showed her true colors, however, rolling her eyes and getting tired of my mom standing up for me. She always thought I needed to get over things, be normal and be quiet, which wasn't sitting well with her. I expected her to be mean, but I wasn't expecting her to be that blatant with her distaste for me. My mom's face turned red as she yelled at her, losing it.

"You could be a human being!" she said. "What gives you the right to talk to her like that?"

The ignorant teacher and my mom got into a scuffle, arguing about my well-being. She knew what was best for me, but the teacher had the nerve to tell her how to parent, making this office argument the equivalent of Mom *WWE.*

Great, just what I needed.

I watched the two of them fighting for what seemed to go on forever, the principal not knowing what to do. This poor lady, very timid and mousy, stood back and thought of what to say while my brown eyes looked at my mom with a sort of cynicism. Now I would get bullied even more, no one wants to be that kid, the one whose mom is overly involved to the point where everyone knows her. I knew she cared about me and she ended up doing so much for the school I was in, but even kids have complicated social standards just as much as adults do; no one wants to be around the overly protected kid because he or she is just lame. Unfortunately, that was my fate, and I was dreading it.

The principal stepped in and thought of a solution to our problem—I was to enter a new class that was neurotypical in nature, but it was much quieter. This was one of the things my mom fought for—she didn't believe in separating me from other children just because I had Autism. All she wanted was for me to have a normal, happy life, so it was off to the quiet class I went. I still remember going through the door of my new class—the kids recognized me as the girl who caused trouble, since it was one of the classes I went to when I was being a distraction. When I sat at my new desk, people were leery of my appearance at first, but I thrived in my new environment. No screaming, no kids throwing markers, just peace and quiet. I didn't completely change—I was still no stranger to hiding in the bathroom whenever we sang and danced to those horrible songs, which inspired my mom to fight for me even more.

Throughout my life, I experienced many forms of therapy to help me with Autism. I couldn't stand loud noise, but one thing that was a big barrier for me was the dreaded fire drill. I couldn't stop covering my ears and hiding under my desk when the thing came on, running away from it like a monster in a horror movie. Every Friday after school, my mom took me to therapy which involved physical, occupational, music, and even art therapy. All this was very expensive, which is why we eventually started doing our own therapies at home. I had weakness in my hands and could barely hold a pencil, so my grandma bought these pencil grips to help me write, reading helped my vocabulary, and listening to music helped me overcome my fear of noise. I distinctly remember listening to opera tapes for three hours straight so I could prepare for the next fire drill.

Therapy is beneficial when it comes to Autism, but nothing happens overnight. It takes a very long time and it all depends on how the child develops. Everyone is made specially and that's what makes us a spectrum. Therapy can help a child, but it will never fix everything. Autism is always within us.

***

Different types of people with Autism may benefit from different things and one thing I enjoyed was pageants. Boys are diagnosed more often than girls and this inspired me to go after my dreams. I didn't have many friends growing up, so like many Autistic kids, I had to go to the one, the only, social skills group. You could probably tell how excited I was.

I protested the whole car ride there, thinking of excuses as to why I shouldn't go. I'm feeling sick, we need to turn around, I have the lumps. Pretty much anything.

I got there and I was saddled with mostly boys, which would be okay if they weren't constantly obsessing over video games; five-year-old me could only put up with that for so long. After three of these groups, I talked to my mom and we started doing pageants because all I wanted was a girl friend to talk to. This wasn't on a whim because I was used to modeling and acting; I was ready for anything. When I got to my first pageant, I felt a little awkward. All the girls were wearing stunning, sparkly dresses and their hair done high and hairsprayed to oblivion, while I looked like I just rolled out of bed while wearing a hand me down dress. I didn't care though, just being at the pageant made me happy!

I competed until I was in the fourth grade, quitting so I could focus on my studies. However, people that knew us told my mom that they saw significant improvements whenever I was around. I was more focused and I could handle noise better, which made sense since the pageant environment is pretty loud. Whenever I was competing when pageants were in a theatre or an arena, I would cover my ears, but I'd gradually not do that anymore because I got used to the environment I was in; it was like magic! Or was it? Was it my sensory wall breaking down?

***

Pageants were not just about winning for me, it was nice to win a crown, which I won many of throughout my life. However, they taught me very important social skills and life skills. One example would be the interview competition, which is my absolute favorite part of any pageant. Not only did the interview competition help with stimming eye contact, but the interview portion teaches young women how to do a real interview in the world, which is useful when you're applying for jobs. I wasn't good at interview at first because I stimmed a lot—always doing stuff with my hands and barely looking the judges in the eyes; another issue that Autistic people deal with. Things were very different from when I was a child—the questions the judges asked became more serious. No longer did they ask "What's your favorite color?" Now the questions grew up, like I was doing.

"Miss Barcellona, why is the new gay marriage law justified?" I smiled, finally an easy question.

"Because everyone's a person, no matter what difference they have."

***

As I got older, I became used to wearing the dresses I hated. It was a challenge at first since I always fought against my mother about them. I guess modeling and acting desensitized me to the uncomfortable feelings. I figured since you will really be wearing anything in both professions, there is no room to criticize your wardrobe. I know that things changed because nowadays, I love dresses, especially vintage ones! I like to wear the vintage ones often and I especially feel pretty when I wear a big, very extra, pageant dress onstage. I know that it makes people happy and I feel happy as well. This is a symbol of all my hard work coming together—if I can go out there wearing a dress with a crown on my head and the biggest of smiles, why can't other Autistic girls? At the end of the day, we all have differences. We are capable just the way we are.

***

One night, I came home after winning another pageant. I was so happy to shed myself of the six contestants' worth of makeup and the dress full of stones weighing heavily down on me. I got into my robe and celebrated yet another victory. My family was very happy for me—I still remember the days when my grandpa loved seeing me win, his smile showing how proud he was of me. My onstage therapy was over for the night and I was ready for bed, but I still thought about how my life was going at this point. Didn't other people do this? Was this normal?

I had a wake-up call when I went to school and people found my new Autism therapy "weird." I guess most people didn't walk around in high heels and dresses—they were scared to sing on stage. I thought about my therapy—things didn't have to be traditional. If someone is happy, we should let them. I let myself be that day as an Autistic adult.

Some people had a fear of being on stage, I had a fear of coming off it.

JEFF SNYDER

A highly motivated and driven individual, Jeff is a relentless self-advocate for Autism awareness. Jeff is active on Facebook and various social media platforms in the effort to promote inclusivity and tolerance within the Autistic and other special-needs related communities and has been featured in various videos discussing such topics. An avid fan-fiction writer and lover, Jeff currently works as a writer on Fimfiction.com and also as a Stop & Shop associate. Jeff lives in Massachusetts and enjoys Disney, My Little Pony, and other fandoms.

Chapter 7: "Living with Autism"

By Jeff Synder

"Everyone is born, but not everyone is born the same. Some will grow to be butchers, or bakers, or candlestick makers. Some even grow up to be good at making Jell-O salad. One way or another, though, every human is unique, for better or for worse."

This was the opening quote to the 1996 film *Matilda* spoken by Danny DeVito. In a way, that is how I start most of my stories on the Autism spectrum. Like what was spoken at the start of the film, I was born, but not the same. I didn't grow up to be a butcher, a baker, or a candlestick maker. I also never grew up to be good at making Jell-O Salad. But in December 1990 at the age of 21 months old, a strange and wonderful phenomenon happened to me. I was diagnosed with Autism.

Like a lot of parents at that time, my own parents were scared of not knowing what Autism really was meant to be. They were scared that I wouldn't amount to anything—they were afraid that I would probably end up not having any friends or not being able to work or even not be able to live on my own once I reached adulthood. However, I didn't even know I was diagnosed with Autism being how young I was. It wasn't until 1998 when at the age of 9 years old, I was featured on a segment of *Nick News* that I finally understood what Autism really is to me. On that day, a news crew from Orlando, Florida came to my house and filmed me for their segment, following me around doing activities such as doing a pretend NASCAR race on my kitchen table.

Even then, I always felt myself to be…different from others. You might say that I was wired differently on a mental level. I lined up my toys in a certain straight line, I collected nothing but Disney movies and watched them nonstop, I would even watch holiday movies during the spring and summer seasons. It was all part of who I am…a person with Autism.

I would go on and on listing, but that would take up a lot of this segment. My contribution to this segment is to identify my strengths and weaknesses of my Autism and share tips and ideas with you all. So let's get started, shall we?

First, if there was one segment of my story that I think people need to know about me is the factor surrounding loud noises. Even though some normal minded people like loud noises, loud noises for me as a kid were very difficult, especially when it came to fire drills that took place in school. To me, fire drills were sort of like kryptonite was to Superman—it made me weak and internally left me a scared and shaking mess!

To a normal thinking person, fire drills were just a way of school life. You never got any advance notice, you just went about your business and then the alarm goes off and chaos ensues. For some, this is a break in routine, a break in the doldrums of the same repetitive nature over and over again. But, to me, it was a very big deal. The only advanced notice I ever got was from a teacher or aide whispering in my ear that we would have a fire drill and from there, I would be taken out of the building before the fire department activated the drill.

The same thing happened with other school drills such as lockdown and bus evacuation drills. It wasn't just loud noises; it was also just the atmosphere of the teacher or bus driver trying to force the students to follow the rules. Just the sheer stern tone in their voices sent chills down my spine. In fact, whenever someone gets angry at me for something, I would always get these chills down my spine, and it's not just in real life as well. There are certain shows and movies that have similar scenes with the kinds of angry people in real life and if they talk in the same manner, I would still get the chills down my spine. If there is any scene from a movie or television show that displays such a scene, I would try to skip over it and I wouldn't care if I was skipping over certain parts of the story.

You might say that I don't like confrontation and that's true to an extent. Confrontation is where you get angry people, and with angry people came the angry, loud tones that made me uncomfortable. But there are times where those situations are unavoidable. You have to face them whether you like it or not.

If I could offer one piece of advice about loud noises, it would be to have an open ear and an open mind for children and adults on the spectrum. They might be diagnosed with a sensory processing disorder or an auditory processing disorder that makes them vulnerable to loud noises.

Next, I would like to talk about the importance of being flexible when it comes to routines. Yes, I get the fact that people with Autism crave routines. Unfortunately, the real world doesn't work the way we Autistic people want. Like everyone else in society, we have to adapt to it.

Take it when I first got a paying job. My job advisor had to hammer into my head that I needed to be flexible when it came to scheduling, for example. I needed to play the games of the employers—to be a part of the team and to pick up the slack when necessary. It didn't matter if I was 18 years old at the time, but it was a lesson that you can't always play by your own rules. If you were to play by your own rules when it came to a job, you would lose that job quicker than you got it. Not every job is going to be accommodating, not every person you work with will have the same personality. Hell, even the general public, the people you serve, won't always have the same personality either. At the time of me writing this statement, I have been in the retail industry for 15 years and you might say that I have been through the wringer on certain days. At times, I was cursed at and yelled at, but it was all in the nature of the business. As someone with sensory processing disorder, I found those kinds of moments to be extremely difficult. Again, it was a message that the world doesn't work the way you want it to.

But another example is being around little kids and families for that matter. Going back to my sensory processing disorder, one of my biggest pet peeves is little kids acting up and their parents having to scold or reprimand them. It drove me bananas and it still does, believe it or not, despite the fact that I now have two nieces that I am trying to be a good role model for.

Now, don't get me wrong, little kids are no different than you or me. However, I've had to teach myself not to be judgmental when it comes to little kids who act up in public. They might even have Autism themselves and their situation is far different than my own.

All this is an example of being flexible and getting out of your comfort zone. Is it hard? Yes, but it's okay as it is a natural part of life. I've learned to cope with these certain situations and intrusions to my sensory processing disorder.

My advice to whoever reads my selection is to be patient and not forceful when trying to get Autistic people to change their routines. It took awhile for me to change my routines from the time I was a kid and guess what? Changing my routines got me, over time, my own apartment that I have been living in since 2015 at the time of this writing.

Speaking of which, this will bring me to my next selection: independence. All my life, I had attempted to secure my shot at independent living. I had lived with my folks until I was 25 years old, but for many on the spectrum, they haven't gotten that chance yet or perhaps they never will.

There might be some of you who might have Autistic children or adults that are just itching to get out and strike on their own. However, like all life changing events, these don't happen overnight. You have to take these things one step at a time.

The first step would be to teach the importance of responsibility. After all, there is a lot more to running an apartment or your own house. First of all, I had to learn how to handle my own laundry and learn how to use a washing machine and a dryer. Secondly, there was also the matter of paying my rent. Before I got my own apartment, I had already taught myself to be responsible with my money. Rather than spending it on useless things that I didn't even need, I taught myself to save my money for things I really needed or wanted. When you get an apartment or house, you have to switch a majority of your finances towards rent or down payments.

For one thing, my folks and I ultimately came down to the decision to apply for social security. It was a pain in the rear, yes, but it was necessary in the long run. It also taught me further that you can't go over a certain amount of money in your bank account.

Before I go on, I want to say that yes, it sometimes is disheartening to hear that you will never be in full control of your finances. Trust me, when I was told that, I was in denial about it. I thought to myself, why should I have no total control over my money? These were the things I didn't really understand and there will be moments where your loved one has that kind of feeling.

Secondly, there is the matter of keeping that flow going in on a weekly basis. If you get a house, apartment, or even a car for that matter, you need to keep the money coming in. Getting a job combined with the social security income at the end of the month should be enough for that extra financial security. As for me, I've focused my finances on my apartment and my travels to various conventions and conferences across the country with a little extra on the side for my own pleasures. Fortunately, my folks swore to back me up financially when I really needed it, much to my relief.

Third is the matter of transportation. I get it, you probably have a loved one on the spectrum who wants to get their own car. I have some friends on the spectrum who have a car or are trying to get one. For one thing, no one can stand being cooped up in their house or apartment all day. However, when it comes to getting a car on the spectrum, some people on the spectrum are very nervous about getting behind the wheel. I happen to be one of those people, to be honest with you. In terms of transportation, I usually take a special needs bus service called GATRA mostly to and from my job or when my folks drive me to wherever I need to go. These strategies have helped me solve my problems in terms of transportation, but it may not work for everyone.

If you are trying to secure a form of transportation for your loved one on the spectrum, you must first approach him or her and ask them if they want to save up for their own car or leave the driving to someone else. What I did was just leave the driving to someone else, but there were limits. For one thing, I sometimes use Uber and Lyft, (where I get Delta Skymiles for every time I ride them), for certain times like airport runs and times where neither my folks or GATRA are available. But these weren't just freewheeling privileges. There was also a matter of safety when it came to using Uber or Lyft as well as finances. One rule you could put in with your loved one is to only use Uber or Lyft during the daytime and not at night. You will never know what you are going to expect when taking a shared ride service. All these are the three most critical goals needed to reach the goal of independence.

But it is very important to remember that I was once in the shoes that your loved ones are now in. Over time, I have come to learn and accept that certain things take a team effort. The world around a person with Autism is very challenging and very scary to both the individual and the individual's loved ones. But one weapon that you must have in your arsenal is patience.

Patience is going to make things a lot easier for you and your loved ones on the spectrum. Even if you are not a patient person, (I must admit that neither me nor my dad are patient people), you will need to learn it at some point because that's just how people with Autism are. We do not mean to hold people back from doing what they need to do, we are just waiting for people to enter into our world.

If I could leave you with one little bit of advice, it would be to not consider Autism as something that is a threat. Everything I have mentioned is meant to help you and your loved one on the Autism spectrum go through life. Remember, you are all a team and you will get through this road…together.

Ron Sandison

Ron Sandison: Ron Sandison works full time in the medical field and is a professor of theology at Destiny School of Ministry. He is an advisory board member of Autism Society Faith Initiative of Autism Society of American and the Art of Autism. Sandison has a Master of Divinity from Oral Roberts University and is the author of *A Parent's Guide to Autism: Practical Advice. Biblical*

Wisdom published by Charisma House and *Thought, Choice, Action*. He has memorized over 15,000 Scriptures including 22 complete books of the New Testament. Sandison speaks at over 70 events a year including 20 plus education conferences. Ron and his wife, Kristen, reside in Rochester Hills, MI, with daughter, Makayla.

Chapter 8: "Autism made numbers my first language; English my second"

By Ron Sandison

Numbers and animals have always been my special interests. I am fascinated by dates and times and can share a million random facts about animals. Like a prairie dog's colony of tunnels, if stretched out, covers over 18-miles in length, or the fact that penguins propose to their mates. In fact, I was so obsessed with prairies dogs as a child, I carried a stuffed animal of a prairie dog from ages 7 to 16. Prairie Pup to this day is the only prairie dog to be officially expelled from the Rochester Hills Public Schools. The special education department told my parents, "At 16, Ron is too old to be carrying a love-worn prairie dog in desperate need of Rogaine." Prairie Pup at 38 is also officially the oldest stuffed animal of a prairie dog.

Even as an adult I still love animals and numbers. I have a pet rabbit, Babs (10), a cat, Frishma (8), and a honey-badger-temperament pup, Rudy (2), who is a mix of

Jack Russell Terrier and Pomeranian. The total age of my pets is a round number of 20. Rudy is the only emotional support pet who needs more emotional support than his Autistic owner—due to his barking meltdowns. Animals also provide me with quirky Autistic moments and stories that I share in my presentations. I speak at over 70 events a year on Autism including 20-plus educational conferences.

Despite his expulsion, Prairie Pup still accompanies me to every speaking event and has traveled around the world from Madagascar to Israel. He even has a friend now—a honey badger. I purchased my first honey badger during my honeymoon in the Windy City. I saw the honey badger in a downtown storefront window. He growled at me and I snarled back; it was love at first sight. When I purchased him, I did not realize that the stuffed animal was created from the YouTube video, *The Honey Badger Don't Care*. When you press his paw, every F-bomb and four-letter obscenity spews out in an angry lisp.

In case you were wondering, I don't bring him to my speaking engagements, (fearing something may brush his paw, causing him to go off before a live audience). The crowd doesn't need to think I'm giving a live demonstration of a meltdown. Instead, I purchased a declawed honey badger from Amazon who travels with me. During COVID-19, I purchased online a handmade lifelike Tasmanian devil from Australia whom I named Taz.

Life has not always been easy—I experienced many social pitfalls and emotion and physical meltdowns in transitioning to adulthood. Numbers and animals always have had a soothing effect on my depression and anxiety. My mind feels at peace when I think visually and with numbers.

My development began at a typical pace. I said my first word, "mommy" at nine months. But at 18 months, I went from saying "mommy" to only "mum." I also lost the ability to interact with my environment and respond appropriately with my peers and maintain eye-contact. About 20% of children with Autism experience a period of regression of previously acquired skills as I did, while many others have a developmental delay with communication and fine motor skills.[1]

My mom realized my communication abilities were severely delayed compared to my two older brothers and

[1] Fred R. Volkmar and Lisa A. Wiesner, *A Practical Guide to Autism: What Every Parent, Family Member, and Teacher Needs to Know 1ˢᵗ Edition* (Hoboken, NJ: John Wiley & Sons, Inc., 209), 253.

took me to the family pediatrician. The pediatrician explained to my mom, "men are like fine wine. You have to give them time; women are like delicate flowers and blossom quickly."

My mom realized the urgency for me to receive services for my delays and advocated for me to receive speech therapy. As a result from ages 2 to 16, I received intensive speech therapy. When I was seven years old, my speech was so delayed, my brother, Chuckie bragged to his friends, "you've got to meet my brother Ronnie. I think he is from Norway since he speaks Norwegian!" For a while, Chuckie and the rest of my family were the only ones able to interpret my language of numbers and animals.

As I entered Kindergarten, the Rochester Community Schools specialists wanted to label me as emotionally impaired. My mom refused this label and informed the professionals, "my son's disability is not emotional but neurological." She diligently researched the top professionals for learning disabilities in the area and paid to have me retested. A neuropsychologist from Henry Ford Hospital confirmed that my disability was indeed neurological and was defined as Autism.

When I was diagnosed with Autism in 1982, only 1 in every 10,000 children in the U.S were diagnosed. Now, 1 out of 59 children is diagnosed and 1 out of 37 males.[2] Since so few children had Autism and I had difficulties making friends, I felt like an endangered species.

The educational specialists warned my parents that I would never read beyond a seventh grade level, attend college, excel in athletics, or have meaningful relationships. But my mom was undeterred by these generalities and instead became more determined to help me succeed in life by developing my unique gifts. She helped me gain self-confidence through creative activities such as painting, drawing, reading, math, and writing short stories.

I now have a bachelor's degree in theology and psychology and a master's of divinity with a minor in Koine Greek from Oral Roberts University. I maintained a 4.0 GPA. I received an athletic scholarship for track and cross-country my freshman year of college. My wife, Kristen, and I were married on December 7, 2012—the anniversary of Pearl Harbor. On March 20, 2016, my daughter, Makayla, was born and just a couple of weeks later, on April 4, 2016, Charisma House published my first

---

[2] The Centers for Disease Control and Prevention (CDC) estimated autism prevalence on April 26, 2018.

book, *A Parent's Guide to Autism: Practical Advice. Biblical Wisdom.*

A cool number fact about my family is we were all born on a Saturday. Five years ago, I met an Autistic savant in the library who calendar-counts. He asked me, "What's your birthday and wife's?"

"May 10, 1975 is my birthday and my wife's birthday is March 6, 1982." After nodding his head 3-times, he instantly replied, "You and your wife were both born on a Saturday. That's good luck!" A year later on March 20, 2016, Makayla was born on a Saturday at 3:13 am—the area code for the city of Detroit.

As a person who loves numbers, experiencing delays was depressing. Every milestone and major event in my life took me longer than my peers and brothers. I graduated from high school at 20, I was 35 years old before I had a long term relationship, 36 when I moved out of my parents' home, 37 when I got married, 41 when I became a father, 42 when my first book was published, and 43 for my second book *Thought, Choice, Action,* and I'll be 45 when my third book *Views from the Spectrum* is published by Kregel.

My mom empowered me to overcome my learning disabilities by quitting her job as an art teacher and becoming a "Ron Teacher." She harnessed my love for animals and numbers to teach me art, reading, and writing. Prairie Pup was instrumental in teaching me social skills and gaining confidence with interacting with girls. The girls in my third grade class created stylish outfits for Prairie Pup; one dressed Prairie in a cowboy costume, another as an astronaut. One even made him a Victorian dress.

In fourth grade, I won the Detroit Edison Drawing contest for Oakland County by creating a poster with Prairie Pup and his furry friends building a tree fort near electrical wires. The caption on the poster stated, "Don't Become a Furry Fried Friend by Building Your Fort Near Power Lines." For the prize, Prairie and I met the captain of the Pistons basketball team, Isaiah Thomas, who was later inducted into the NBA Hall of Fame.

Even with all my success in art, academics, athletics, and developing friendships—I still struggled after college for ten years with gainful employment.

In 2005, I found myself unemployed and unable to find stable employment for three years despite having a master's degree. I was previously employed full time at a large church in Oakland Township as a ministry intern and part-time as a youth pastor at a church in Highland. Due to the downfall in Michigan's economy and recession, I was let go from both churches.

For the next three years, I experienced unsteady employment, working four months at Corky's Skateboard Shop for $5.25 an hour, five months at a moving company, and the remainder at Cross Roads for Youth as a youth specialist. I felt confused and depressed.

While in prayer, God revealed to me seven principles to apply to my life to be successful and I wrote them in my journal entry on April 13, 2006—notice the month being Autism Awareness Month:

Seven Skills

1. Seek first to understand, then to be understood.

2. No monotone—Ron, you sound like a robot. (Two different girls told me this).

3. Timing of words. Proverb 15:23, "A person finds joy in giving an apt reply—and how good is a timely word!"

4. Have eye contact when talking to people.

5. Pronounce "TH" and "L" words by using the proper tongue movements.

6. Pray and seek the Lord.

7. Develop a strategy for people skills by imitating friends who have those skills.

Near the completion of my three years of darkness, after a church service, a congregant gave me a piece of paper with a handwritten message and told me, "I believe this is a message for you." It stated, "God has a job for you in a field that you would never expect and this will prepare you for the ministry." A week later, I was hired at a mental health hospital as a psychiatric care specialist (PCS) where I would be working with aggressive, acute-psychotic male patients.   During this season, I also focused on developing my people skills, learning relationship skills from church single groups and online dating. Four relationship skills I learned through dating were:

1. *Numbers are important*—if a girl or guy breaks your heart, don't give up—there are plenty of fish in the sea. I went on at least one date with over 300 different women before I met my wife. The only difference between a successful person and a failure is a successful person rises one more time than they fall.

2. *Be interested but not hovering.* People with Autism in dating have a tendency to become obsessive and totally focused on their desired partner. This extreme focus can

help an individual be successful in college or a career, but in dating it will lead to a restraining order.

3. *It's not you, it's them.* If a person you are dating cheats on you, this person will also cheat on the next person he or she dates. It's not something you did, it's who that person is—a cheater. Don't let this heartbreak hold you back from meeting a faithful woman or man.

4. *Seek first to understand, then to be understood.* I love to tell stories and can become obsessed on the topic of my special interests—the Bible and psychology. I often fail to listen to others. A female from a church group, whom I had dated for three months, decided to end our brief relationship. After I rambled on for an hour telling her my humorous stories, I failed to take time to listen to her horrible epic battle with her washing machine. Her last words to me were, "You never listen to me when I talk!"

Over the next three years, I mastered these four concepts. I read hundreds of books and articles on the subject of relationships and went on at least one date with over 300 different women in my quest for a wife. I averaged three to four dates a week. I took notes after each date to improve my relationship skills and be equipped to interpret body language. It became my new special interest—women. I developed my social skills and became conscious of other people's felt needs in conversations.

On May 11, 2010, I met my beautiful wife, Kristen, at a coffee shop. Our relationship was steady and after two-and-a half years of dating, we were married. This past year marked 12.5 years of gainful employment in the mental health field and 17 years at Destiny Ministry School as a professor of theology. I also founded an organization five years ago called Spectrum Inclusion which empowers young adults with Autism for employment and independence.

Three tips I share with young adults who struggle with employment are:

1. *Most people find employment by personal connections.* While working part-time for Comfort Keepers, I overheard one of the staff at the nursing home state, "I work at Havenwyck Hospital." I told this staff member, "I submitted my résumé to Havenwyck four months ago and never heard back!" She advised me, "Tomorrow, go and ask for my supervisor and he will hire you. I'll call him tonight." The next day, I went to the hospital and asked to meet with her supervisor—he hired me.

2. *Employment comes to those who diligently seek.* Again, employment is a numbers game like dating. I encourage young adults to never quit or become discouraged in their quest for employment. If you keep searching for a job and improve your abilities, you will be employed. It may not be your dream job, but continue to be faithful, keep improving your skills, and learn lessons in your current workplace. This will ultimately lead you to a career you enjoy.

3. *Find a mentor who is successful in the career you desire.* Pick a mentor who is understanding of your disability, who is patient, and who has been working in the field for at least a few years. Watch and learn from him. Proverbs 27:17 says, "As iron sharpens iron, so one person sharpens another." My mentor was TV evangelist Dr. Jack Van Impe, who had over 15,000 Scriptures memorized. He inspired me to also memorize over 15,000 verses. During the summer of my senior year at Oral Roberts University, I was able to be mentored under Dr. Van Impe. Through this internship, I learned the skills required for operating an international ministry and was able to develop my ministry skills.

Numbers and animals were keys to my success. Learn how Autism affects you and how it makes you unique. This knowledge will enable you to be successful in relationships and the workplace. Living with Autism will be difficult and lonely, but keep moving forward and use the gifts God has given you—don't lose heart. As Charles Spurgeon said, "By perseverance, the snail made it on the ark."

Jesse Saperstein

Jesse A. Saperstein is a best-selling author, autism advocate and motivational speaker. He is considered one of the most respected leaders in the Anti-Bullying movement of his generation. Jesse also has a form of autism called Asperger's syndrome (AS) that gives individuals some profound talents and challenges.

After graduating from Hobart and William Smith Colleges in 2004 with a BA degree in English, Jesse set out to conquer the 2,174-mile Appalachian Trail to benefit the Joey DiPaolo AIDS Foundation. He began hiking from Georgia to Maine on March 9, 2005 and successfully completed the journey on October 18, 2005, raising more than $19,000 for children to attend summer camp who had contracted HIV/AIDS through prenatal transmission.

Shortly after his hike ended, Jesse was exposed to some of the harsh realities of living as an adult on the autism spectrum and was treated with fear by members of the community who did not understand. His decision to write a book was an opportunity to escape these realities and advocate for his peers who are not always granted a voice.

Jesse's story, "Atypical: Life with Asperger's in 20 1/3 Chapters," was published by Penguin Group (USA) in April 2010 and immediately became a popular memoir due to its practical advice and humor. After receiving a grant from the Anderson Center for Autism (ACA) in Staatsburg, New York, Jesse completed his first skydiving jump in front of his community in an effort to eradicate bullying. "Free-Falling to End Bullying in 2012" is now a popular video on YouTube: www.youtube.com/jessesaperstein. Jesse visits schools on a regular basis and has been successful with wiping out bullying or at least dramatically alleviating it with every presentation. He was part of the "Keeping it Real" project with New York University (NYU) that helped introduce a new anti-bullying curriculum to New York City public schools. The web page is: www.projectkeepitreal.com He has spoken in front of the United Nations and the Mall of America in Minneapolis, MN among many other places.

His second book, "Getting a Life with Asperger's: Lessons Learned on the Bumpy Road to Adulthood" was released on Tuesday, August 5, 2014 and focuses on surviving the difficult transition into adulthood if someone has an autism spectrum disorder.

Jesse moved to Albany in June 2015 to live in his first apartment as an independent adult, and serves as the Media and Activities Liaison for the College Experience that is run by Living Resources, Inc. The College Experience is a program that gives individuals with disabilities the ability to attend a mainstream college with a modified curriculum and provides life skills as well as employment training, which can be found on www.thecollegeexperience.org in addition to some of Jesse's blog entries.

His long-term goal is addressing the National Democratic Convention to advocate for oppressed US citizens and other Americans trying to reach their potential who have disabilities. On the date of Tuesday, April 2, 2019 Jesse had the honor of being included as one of the thirty-plus American heroes profiled within the anthology, "American Spirit" produced by New York Times Bestselling authors, Taya Kyle and Jim DeFelice. On Wednesday, January 22, 2020 Jesse appeared on the *Dr. Phil* television show after successfully pitching producers to advocate for his friend, David Elmore Smith, who was in dire need of resources to combat his morbid obesity. He has recently worked with the CEO of the American Red Cross to replenish the blood supply in hospitals, especially if it is the antibody-enriched plasma harvested from survivors of COVID-19.

Chapter 9: "Letting Go"

By Jesse Saperstein

As a child, life seemed pretty damn good when ignorance was bliss. I did not know about differences or those that I possessed, which would eventually ruin my life in prolonged spurts until life finally settled down to a bearable existence well into adulthood. It helped when I was growing up that there was consistency and routine. For example, the perennial buds always pushed out of the soil in late spring in the same raised ranch that I lived in until the age of 16. All four of my grandparents remained alive until the age of 11 when they started falling victim to the vulnerabilities that come with a long life such as cancer and Alzheimer's disease. Both my mother and father remained together, which avoided shaking up my fragile state of mind with change that could not be put back together in its former glory. I cringe while imagining the behavioral challenges that would have been inevitable if I were forced to divide time between two houses.

Until the bullying truly started with a vengeance and stayed around in different forms, I remember being a very happy child and did not mind that there were not many friends aside from the playdates that my mother arranged. It is interesting how we do not pine over and miss the things we do not have. But I was perfectly content with the occasional video game orgasm at the arcade, cartoons, trips to Ocean City in Maryland, and other forms of childhood euphoria. One of my favorite pastimes growing up was bouncing a basketball at the hoop too tall for an eleven-year-old boy while imagining that I was traveling the cavernous colonies carved out by the ants that made their home in the cracks of my sidewalk cement. I probably was attracted to this fantasy because it seemed like a perfect world in which everybody was accepted and had a place that was vital toward making the society function. It was similar to Jim Henson's *Fraggle Rock* with the indolent Fraggles and hardworking Doozers coexisting. As long as there was a working Queen, it would go on forever. But nothing goes on forever.

I have been conditioned to hate and vilify changes that are synonymous with life. Transitions were always synonymous with fixing what was previously working fine. In fifth grade, I left a haven in which there was no bullying and life was wonderful due to a caring teacher who knew how to deal with my occasional outbursts or attempts to be funny. One time she reacted to a "very stupid question" about farting during a lecture on the digestive system by explaining it In dry, scientific terms instead of letting me succeed in "rattling her cage" as she put it while recounting the experience when I was substitute teaching in her middle school. But this year ended as school years always do.vI was thrown in the jungle of sixth grade in which we were ferried from class to class all day long and being flamboyantly eccentric was social suicide. Sometimes, the bad experiences eventually became euphoric, however. By the end of high school, I was mostly accepted by the other students and truly came out of my shell in an epic way. There were even dates with young ladies—one of them being the woman of my dreams! Despite having been a special education student throughout high school, I was miraculously starting to excel in math, science, and art, which had always been my weakest subjects. It was no wonder that I despised looking at colleges and being reminded in my junior year that everything would fade away. Sure enough, my clean slate and the honeymoon period at Hobart and William Smith Colleges starting in the year 2000 was quickly demolished with the erratic behavior that is sometimes synonymous with being on the Autism spectrum. The better part of four years was plagued with nicknames such as Sketchy Jesse, Scary Jesse, Running Jesse, and other monikers. In all honesty, if the pandemic had to happen in my lifetime, it would have been a godsend if it had destroyed one of these brutal semesters to send me home for a very prolonged summer vacation. In those days there was no such thing as Zoom and the primitive version of the internet could not have supported online learning the same way as today. Nobody likes contending with a pandemic, but in the spirit of the glass being half-full, it is accurate to assert that sometimes the worst things happen at the best possible times. There were surely some wonderful parts of college such as receiving the Award for Excellence in the humanities and studying in Bath, England. But it was not enough to compensate for the times when there was overpowering loneliness coupled with the fear it would never end.

One aspect of my life that has both kept me going and driven me to the brink of insanity is the inability to "let go" and "move on." This proved to be the most vital resource after college when I set off to complete the Appalachian Trail starting in March 2005. The Appalachian Trail stretches forward like a never-ending green tunnel all the way from Georgia to Maine for 2,174-miles—it feels like it goes on forever. The reason I completed this hike is because of the knowledge of what waited for me at the very end if I were to come home prematurely due to not being able to cut it as a long-distance hiker. It would not have been pretty at all. After the two weeks of bliss from being reunited with all the amenities that are not accessible in the woods, I would have descended in my own nightmare. The failure would have gnawed at my self-esteem like a beaver. My thoughts would be consumed with returning to get the monkey off my back. My family would have insisted in vain that I let it go and get on with my life. Ultimately, I would have either dwelled on it forever or eventually returned to finish the job.

Completing this physical journey for over half-a-year was one of the hardest and yet easiest feats I have ever taken on in my 38 years of life. It was certainly difficult due to the relentlessness of the task. There are moments of extreme physical discomfort such as chafing that makes your groin area feel like it was blasted by a belt sander! Hiking 10 to 15 miles almost every single day creates an overwhelming fatigue that makes it feel like one has been drugged. On the other hand, the mileage is not at the mercy of the free will of other people who have the power to say "no" or find something wrong. The mileage is an inanimate object that will respond positively to one's effort. Every single day, the beast is chipped away because there is a little more behind than before. The journey also raised nearly twenty thousand dollars for a pediatric AIDS foundation that is now defunct because of the economic crash of 2008. It taught me to be proud of the fact that it is not possible to let things go. I would not be who I am if it were easily possible to let go and move on.

One aspect about me that has not become any better over the past few years is an extreme phobia of unnecessary waste. Going into restaurants can be a debilitating experience, considering they very seldom listen to my pleas to not give me a plastic straw or anything plastic period. I will ask for a ceramic, washable mug "for here," only to receive a disposable cup. It happens so often that I honestly think they did it on purpose due to not wanting to wash dishes. I do my best to be polite but firm. It is explained to them how important this is in my life. Other people can do what they want and pollute the oceans with plastic. But in my personal life, I have the right to not be forced to make choices that destroy our fragile environment. Something that I have long advocated for is the servers giving the patrons straws already wrapped because it is just a reflex for them after doing the same thing a thousand times all week long. This way, I can nicely hand it back and politely remind them that we just talked about this three minutes ago. No harm will be done and we could all pretend this never happened. Deep down, I know that I am right. If everybody were exactly like me, there would be no global warming and the oceans would be free of plastic sewage. But anger issues as a result of so many people ignoring my reasonable requests to not poison the world are a huge issue when going out in public. For example, I nearly lost composure at a company picnic when I brought my own plate to avoid using the styrofoam products. After trying to explain for what seemed like five minutes to the vendor that I have my own plate and to please put the meatball sandwich on my environmentally friendly plate, he took it off the disposable plate and then threw the styrofoam plate in the garbage. In so many words, I asked him to never do that to me ever again. "The reason I bring my own plate is so that very thing does not happen!" For me, this is a really big deal even though I understand it is not as though anyone had died. I will keep advocating for myself and would even divorce the woman of my dreams if she insisted on only using disposable plates and plastic silverware all the time to avoid washing dishes. I would either compromise and offer to take care of the dishes forever or I would leave the marriage. This is how critical this belief is to me and am never going to change. But I am able to compromise, back off, and put things on a backburner when there is no choice!

For example, bus boys at weddings and bar/bat mitzvahs are my mortal enemies! It truly seems as though they do not care or have any consideration for whether people are done with their meals. They do not want to be there because for them, it is just a job. A means to an end. There is a good chance most of your delicious steak dinner will be in the garbage when you leave to use the bathroom or leave the table for a few minutes to greet a relative. I promised my sister, Dena, that I would refrain from making a scene at her wedding if this should happen and would pretend not to be enraged by such stupidity. If I were making the rules at a wedding, every guest would be given a shot glass that is painted red at the bottom. Whenever it is turned upside-down on the plate, it would mean the dinner is done and the food may be thrown in the garbage.

It was not exactly Sophie's choice about what to do. Shall I make a scene and embarrass my poor sister on the most important day of her life, or accept the inevitable spilt steak dinner? I meant…spilt milk?

During the pandemic, I am haunted by brutal memories such as the fact that I quit the clarinet in the fourth grade or never attempted to learn the piano. I would-have, should-have, and could-have punched one of my sociopathic childhood tormentors in the face to shave off my suffering in youth. Damn! I would have landed in a lion's den of trouble, but it would have been worth it. The worst that would have happened was earning a paid five-day vacation from middle school where I would bask in the glow of *Eureeka's Castle*, *David the Gnome,* and all those wondrous children's shows that only premiered during school hours. Most brilliantly, I would have been left with the satisfaction of having fought back and how good it must have felt. Being a model student was all I had back then as well as having a clean disciplinary record. But this provides little comfort as an adult when the demons come late at night.

As a 38-year-old adult, I am very pleased to let everybody know that I have lived two extremely different lives as someone on the Autism spectrum. There is the life encompassing most of my youth of loneliness made worse by bouts of flamboyantly eccentric behavior probably geared toward seizing negative attention. For example, one time in gym class I farted very loudly on purpose! There were even periods of borderline stalking due to the inability to handle being ignored or rejected. All I can say is that at the time, I thought it was the right thing to do. The same unrelenting determination that propelled me throughout the Appalachian Trail did not fare so well when directed toward other human beings with the power to push against these efforts just as tenaciously and occasionally try to take "further action," if you know what I mean. I always thought things would change someday if I never gave up. Only rarely did the young woman come around to change her mind, however.

But even with the ladies, I am still unable to completely let go or move on. One of the things that has always driven me wild with misery are when others have severed contact with me without warning or provocation. There were a couple of ladies who were once my entire world. Things never progressed romantically and I was able to accept this unchangeable reality. But when these angels were around, they lifted me to the moon and beyond the stars. They were not perfect in any way, shape, or form. One of them was prone to moments of extremely inconsiderate behavior, for example. I remember the time when she invited me to attend her stepson's anti-bullying seminar at a karate studio. Not only did she fail to show up with the boy, but she also ignored my phone calls all day long to find out what happened as though it were my fault for showing up at the designated place and time. But I was able to brush off these rare flare ups of a mental disease that I refer to as "assholicitius." One day, she disappeared without warning forever and I have not heard from her since. In order to deal with not being capable of letting go, I have created a tactic called, "Incremental Backing Off." This refers to portioning one's obsessions into manageable micro-explosions. Perhaps I am telling you this to justify my behavior. Or maybe it is for reasons greater than myself. One day, there could be a younger peer who is dealing with ravages of being compelled to hold on for dear life. I will never tell him or her to "let go" unless the consequences will be brutal. I would explain the facts of life and how much worse it can get when the obsessions take over like a viral force. "Perhaps we should try putting this on a backburner for a month and then see what happens…" The fact is there are no more accusations of stalking or threats to get the authorities involved if I do not stop pushing. It is enough to feel very proud of all this progress.

Life did not get much better until the age of 34. Nothing is perfect, but it is certainly much closer to perfect than in my previous years that were similar to an ongoing Catch-22. People often want to know how it feels to live with Asperger's syndrome. This is going to be a different answer for each person, but for the majority of my nearly forty years on the Autism spectrum, life with Asperger's was synonymous with never being able to win! The breaks that seemed to come to my neurotypical peers did not grace me with nearly as much frequency. Having Asperger's is never being able to solve any problems. Or what is even more frustrating is when a huge problem is solved only to create a new one it is place like the head of the mythological Hydra. I remember working on my first book with Penguin Group (USA) back in 2008-2009. The writing process was plagued with procrastination for at least three months when barely a word was written. It was more about wanting it to be perfect and not starting until I knew exactly what to write and an assurance it would guarantee a stellar book. At the time, there was not enough inspiration and creative energy to crank it out with gusto. Somehow, things came together at the very last minute. Not literally the last minute, mind you. There were three months left of the deadline and perhaps eight chapters had been written at that point. It was not as though nothing had been completed, although my family was on my case all the time telling me how disappointed they were that so much time had been wasted. They were right to be so hard on me. There was not a ton of time left, but there was enough time. It was enough time to gauge that if I were to complete only one chapter a week, I would still be in excellent shape. An entire book came together in the most wonderous fashion with about ten thousand extra words handed in by the deadline. The editor and my family were quite happy. I started placing new chapters on the kitchen table at six o'clock in the morning and my father, Lewis, had said to my mother, "He is back."

The inability to let go torments me to no end even when something works out and is saturated with achievement after a rough start. I was beating myself up internally until it came time to write the second book with

Penguin Group (USA). Life had handed me what is craved by every shamed athlete or defeated public figure. The ability to redeem oneself with a second chance. This time I was going to spuckle stown...I mean...to pound that baby out and kick its butt like no author had before. There was a generous deadline once again of maybe six months, but my deadline would be five months. This time, my family was not as harsh because they knew I would pull it off despite the inevitable bumps. The goal this time was to not make it perfect but create a goal of four thousand words per chapter. It would not make a difference if it was the worst chapter in humanity. All that would matter is that something would exist that did not the previous day. What happened is the Godzilla-like monster that was defeated starting in 2013 was only to be replaced by a first draft that was turned in early and needed a ton of work. One of the chapters was so bad, it had to be thrown away by the editor. But my incredible editor was quite ginger and showed mercy. Over time, the terrible first draft became better with editing because there was something that now existed. Living with Asperger's is understanding that victory comes in knowing that the new problem is less of a problem than the one that has just been eradicated. I have learned how to advocate for myself when criticism seems unfair and the person does not appreciate the work that has been put into getting to this point. For example, not everybody was impressed by my tenacity to control what comes out of my mouth and sculpting my words to be socially appropriate. Sometimes, their well-meaning comments are: "You try too hard" or "You cannot worry about getting into trouble so much that you are not firm enough and are too wishy-washy." These are actual things people have said to me to rain on the parade of victory that came with learning how to exhibit self-control. The fact is that no matter how much time has passed, I am terrified of getting into trouble because back in 2006, I lost two careers in a very short period of time and it took nearly ten years to bounce back and reclaim my professional reputation.

These days, I have a comfortable existence as the Media and Activities Liaison for the College Experience in Albany that is run by Living Resources, Inc. and the College of Saint Rose in Albany, New York. Some of my duties include being the social media blogger, the Activities Coordinator, the Volunteer Coordinator, a creative writing instructor, a self-advocacy instructor, and occasionally a driver when they need someone to help out at a moment's notice. The start was incredibly rocky as most of my life transitions. Success eventually came to fruition as a result of always going above and beyond the line of duty. It is a practice that I refer to as "Asperger's Insurance." It is the knowledge that eventually a mistake will be made and hopefully the dozens of things done right prior to the mistake will make an enormous difference. Every redemptive act performed prior to the setback will wash away any neurotic feelings of guilt within myself or annoyance from supervisors. For example, one time during Yom Kippur, I decided to be with my family in Pleasant Valley, New York and completely forgot about my responsibility to pick up one of the program's alumni who was volunteering at the American Red Cross that day. After calling the supervisor who was understanding, I took the action of arranging a taxi company to transport the individual home while using my own money. Instead of being angry, the supervisor was impressed. I am very blessed to be working with people these days who save their overreacting for when I do something right instead of always finding something wrong.

There are still obsessions that I try to hold onto because it is not fair to let go of everything. One of my favorite things to do in the entire world is watching old clips of cartoon nostalgia from the days of yore and yesteryear when life seemed simpler. Nobody can take this away from me, especially if I get all of my work completed while indulging in this silliness. It is a tactic that I refer to as "Prodonsense." In other words, it is the act of combining productivity with utter nonsense. If the dishes may be completed while watching a YouTube *SpongeBob* musical number on the phone, then that is just awesome in more ways than one! Some things have been forced to die their inevitable death such as trick-or-treating on Halloween. This cherished childhood ritual had to finally stop at age 31 because of the commitments within the adult world and having to move to Albany two years later, where they would not have been so tolerant to see a man in his thirties collecting candy at random houses. I guess there comes a point when there is no disPUTE that it is no longer CUTE! Carving jack o' lanterns also had to end due to the fact it takes all day long and my apartment complex does not allow lit candles. I simply do not believe in battery operated candles because of being a Halloween purist. But I will always believe in the magic of Halloween! In fact, the day will come when most public schools cave into the pressures of over-the-top political correctness. They will ban Halloween or replace it with a pathetic compromise such as "The Fall Festival" or "Crazy Sock Day." When this real-life horror happens, I am hoping the children will band together and turn the tables on the adult world by sneaking costumes into school and then making their bodies go limp so they have to be literally dragged out of class in their Halloween costumes. There are times when we must realize that trying to please everybody only makes a tiny minority of people happy while driving ourselves crazy in the process. I would make an excellent elementary school principal because if two families threatened to take legal action against me for permitting Halloween because it is against their religions, I would happily say, "Go for it! As much as I would love to break the hearts of every child in this school, I would prefer you instead get a life and realize that despite what may have happened hundreds of years ago in Salem, Massachusetts, Halloween is the shining jewel of childhood!"

The one thing raging within my soul right now is an obsession with creating an Emergency National

Convalescent Plasma campaign. I am trying to rally the nation and some of our top celebrities to saturate the hospitals with this liquid gold that is going to help get patients off of ventilators. Perhaps this will assuage every regret, failure, and justify dwelling on so many things that more sensible people would have dropped a very long time ago. My attitude is that if one wants to go good within humanity, they must believe they are saving the entire world. If we do not have this attitude, nobody will bother because they will say, "What's the point." Blood drives have been a part of my life for 21 years because they were a haven when the constant bullying would finally come to an abrupt halt. At the blood drives, if I were to accidentally say the wrong thing or commit an act of social awkwardness, it would not be a big deal. After having made countless donations, there is no more fear of needles and I am attempting to turn this into a platform in which I have filmed YouTube videos that involve delivering motivational speeches while hooked up to the phlebotomy machine. Most recently, I have been acknowledged by the American Red Cross in a blog entry and communicated with the CEO down in Washington, D.C. The inability to let go also led me to contact *The Dr. Phil Show* to help save the life of my good friend, David Elmore Smith. This all began last January when something forced me to write a proposal to a producer about my friend's journey of being morbidly obese, losing four hundred pounds, and then tragically regaining it back. A higher power told me that something bad was going to happen if this email was not sent. It would either be his death or some other horrific thing that would prevent him from receiving the resources necessary to reverse the years of damage. This could not have been the type of show that Dr. Phil could conduct from his kitchen and perhaps the pandemic pandemonium would have been the final straw for David's sad existence. It is now, more than ever, that I am pleased to have the complete inability to let go and move on. But if others on the spectrum are exactly like me, I want them to know they can still move forward. They will find ways to justify how they are because it will slowly but surely change the world!

Monica MacDonald

Monica is a classic Canadian wild child. She is an excitable, optimistic autistic who is unapologetically open about her thoughts and feelings. She encourages others to engage in that same freedom. Monica is passionate about neruo-diversity and self awareness. She is a former ABA therapist but does not practice professionally any longer due to moral conflict. Monica works primarily teaching parents to create an environment for their child that sets them up for success. She also helps kids to practice emotional regulation and coping skills post trauma. She loves water and barns and creatures and trees. You can often find her laying in a field somewhere pondering life.

Feel free to email Monica with any questions or comments about the content she has shared.

Chapter 10: "Becoming Seen and Heard"

By Monica MacDonald

My Name is Monica MacDonald. My two older brothers and myself were raised in a small town in Ontario, Canada. My parents are phenomenal. They truly and deeply love us. They are also conservative. Their fierce love and acceptance of us meant that my "differences" went unnoticed. Their nature also left them a little less reformed in the mental health department. They probably thought they just landed some weird kids. Being undiagnosed until adulthood had its benefits and drawbacks. I'm excited to discuss my experience with you and I thank you for wanting to hear from real Autistics about Autistic life and culture. Keep in mind; I am ONE person, so hearing some of my story means you know part of ONE story. Just as every neurotypical is different, so is every neurodivergent.

I was a pretty happy go lucky kid. I was all about bouncing and jumping and laughing. I loved to be cuddled and tickled. I loved to chat with my family and close friends. I was, and am, a lover of all things water. Pools. Puddles.

Ponds. Fountains. Rivers. Oceans. Lakes. Waterfalls. You name it, I want in it. Luckily for my parents, we had a pool, so it was easy enough for them to send me outside to burn off my abundance of energy. In the winter, snow would suffice. I loved Legos. I loved setting up, but not playing with, my Barbie house. We rode bikes and climbed trees and played sports in our huge backyard. We were read to and had family movie nights. We ate dinner together at the table every night. We roughhoused and laughed together.

My mother kept us home with her until we were five. My dad travelled a lot for work, sometimes two to three weeks at a time. My mom was our primary caregiver. Those first five years were pretty chill. I kind of just did what I wanted most days. Played outside. Baked with Mom. Played cards. Did puzzles. Coloured. Watched TV. When we went to the grocery store together, I always felt disoriented there, so I stayed close to Mom and stayed quiet/zoned out until we were done. I had play dates with cousins and family friends. I felt like a "normal kid."

Somewhere in my early school years, my outlook on life changed. I began to have days that I felt detached from my family and community. As I grew up, those times of loneliness increased. I started to recognize that others often saw my happiness and joy as exaggerated or over the top. I was confused. Why was I a loser? Why did people laugh at me? Why didn't I have friends my age? (Most of my friends were older and a few younger). Confusion turned into anxiety. I became concerned with my weight at age six. I was a super strong and active kid. But maybe people don't like me because I am fat? The anxiety carried over to academic performance. I am great at math and geography; I was not so great at spelling or speaking French. Maybe people don't like me because I'm not smart enough? I was raised in a Christian home, so the anxiety spilled into my relationship with church and God. Maybe people don't like me because I'm that kid? My mind was in chaos. I found it hard to focus in class; worried about all the things I didn't understand about my peers and myself. I didn't like it when I didn't know why they were laughing or when they would run away from me. At about age seven or eight, I stopped reaching out socially. I had a few friends and the risk of rejection was too high to try for more.

I was raised in a culture where kids are to be "seen and not heard." That doesn't really fly for the excitable Autistic kid who is unapologetically open about their thoughts and feels. I started to see myself as "too much" at about age four to six. My dad is hyper sensitive to touch and sound. I was a loud and touchy kid. I didn't understand his needs, nor did he, mine. Not really knowing what would upset my dad caused anxiety at home too. He would become loud and angry if my brothers and I were arguing, but the same thing would happen if I was bouncing around or laughing. I didn't understand the rules or why it was "bad" to be happy. I felt rejected sometimes, but mostly I knew that he was for me. He loves me deeply. I was, and still am, "little girl." I'd climb up in his lazy-boy and we'd watch shows or take naps or play silly little games together. He'd rub my back and I'd rub his head. He was this big, huge, soft, cuddly safety net when I was calm/quiet. But that was rare, and I struggled to keep my happy emotions inside. I needed a physical outlet for expression and didn't know of one that my family deemed acceptable. So I spent a lot of time being told to calm down/quiet down when I was really just in a good mood. It was a mood killer for sure.

I had consistent and recurrent nightmares. I didn't sleep through the night from ages 3 to age 14. I would often go climb in bed with my amazing big brother after a horrific dream, trying to feel some sort of safety within his protective reach. I was terrified of going to bed and would meltdown most nights. Because of my parents conservative nature, my crisis state was viewed as disobedience or as a tantrum, which meant I was usually left alone—screaming or sobbing in panic.

I was a particular kid. I liked certain numbers (1,3,5,7). I was picky with clothing texture and style. I didn't like to be touched unless I initiated it. I hated the sound of whistling. I loved smacking my back on the backrest of the seat in the car. I could not stand being hot. I didn't like people touching my stuff or helping me with things. My mother, by nature, is a helper. She performs acts of service to show love. This made for lots of conflict between her and I. She would clean our rooms while we were at school sometimes. My brothers so appreciated this. I, however, would lose my ever-loving mind. Full-blown, destroying my room, screaming, stomping, throwing my body on the floor, out of control, meltdown. But again, this was seen as a tantrum. Rude. Disrespectful. Unappreciative. In those crisis moments, I didn't have the language to explain my needs. I didn't even fully understand my needs, so I was punished for my behaviour. These kinds of meltdowns weren't super regular but frequent enough that I learned if it happened, I'd be in trouble. At this point around ages seven to nine, I learned to internalize those uncontrollable feelings. I would go hide under my blankets and bite my hands or rip out chunks of my hair, desperately trying to release the tension and chaos I felt. I was alone and misunderstood by the people who I knew loved me desperately.

I reached out to my mother for help when I was about 10. I came to the kitchen, (where she spent hours baking sweets for us and fresh home cooked meals for each night), crying and begging her for help. I said, "I'm so angry and I don't know how to make it stop." Unfortunately, my mom didn't know how to make it stop either and I don't think she recognized the desperation and severity of my plea. She turned around and calmly said "go scream into or punch your pillow." This felt so inadequate to me and I never asked her for help coping again.

I love my family. I do not however, love large family gatherings. They are overwhelming. The social requirements. The touching. The talking. The eating together. It's all way too much. As a kid, I would often go find somewhere alone to play quietly. For my first five years, this was behind my grandpa's bar. We grandkids weren't allowed back there, for obvious reasons, because of the breakables and alcohol. But Grandpa always turned a "blind eye" to me being back there. I just sat and played quietly by myself. Or if I couldn't get myself alone, I would sit on my dad's knee safe inside his big arms. Oftentimes, these two comforting situations were met with resistance from my aunts, claiming that I was a "baby" or "whiny" because I was either breaking the rules being behind the bar or by disrupting adult time sitting with Dad. As I got older, I think my dad noticed my need for him wasn't reducing at the same rate as my cousins' need for their dads. He became softened to my requests for him. He turned me away less and ignored his sisters more.

One of my main "problem behaviours" was my refusal to eat almost any meat. I would eat any vegetable, any fruit; I could take or leave carbs. But meat has been a struggle my whole life. I would sit at the table until bedtime just waiting. The texture was too much. There was too much unknown. To this day, I will only eat meat if I pick it apart with my fingers first. My eating also changes drastically with anxiety. Just because I liked something yesterday does not mean I am eating it next week. The more force that is applied to the issue, the harder it gets to break the cycle. I have gone more than a week without eating on several occasions because the thought of food in my mouth is repulsive. I can counteract this pattern by drinking green juice, then smoothies, then baby food, then raw veggies—slowly working back towards a somewhat typical diet. This can happen several times a year depending on the stresses of life. It's a process. But I'm okay with it and it goes better when everyone else is too.

The dentist was a huge anxiety trigger for me. I was a tough kid with a high pain tolerance. But I dreaded the dentist. I would sit through it, crying in agony. Telling the dentist he was hurting me, to no avail. What we didn't know then was that I have EDS (Ehlers-Danlos Syndrome), which can reduce the impact of anesthetic. So when the dentist was adamantly telling my parents I couldn't feel anything, I could. Again, I felt misunderstood, knowing they, (Mom and Dad) were there for me but not able to tell them what I needed. Another one of my EDS traits is loose joints/dislocations. Those started at 16 months but my family doctor and the specialist agree it wasn't concerning and I would grow out of it by age five. That didn't happen. Then they said by puberty. That didn't happen. There were some additional notable EDS traits through childhood but no one ever put them together as a diagnosable genetic condition and separately, they seem like minimally life changing issues. At age 21 when I was in the ER getting stitches, I explained to the doctor the freezing wouldn't work and to just do them anyways. The doctor was shocked and amused and suggested I be tested for EDS. This was the first time I'd heard of it.

I started fainting when I was 12. The doctor ran some tests but concluded that it was just part of puberty and I would grow out of it too. But I never did. I just learned to cope with it. It wasn't super frequent and seemed fairly inconsequential until July 2019. That day, I collapsed because my blood pressure dropped so low my heart stopped. I sustained a brain injury and was admitted to the cardiac intensive care unit for 5 days due to atrial fibrillation following the event. I was diagnosed with vasovagal syncope. The reason this is relevant is because EDS and VVS are part of dysautonomia and that is frequently comorbid with Autism. Had someone diagnosed me with one, it's much more likely they would have recognized the others also.

At 11 years old, I had met my breaking point with school. It had always been a struggle. I had a hard time focusing in classroom environments, (30 kids). I was bored. Music and gym class specifically were always overwhelming, but I didn't know what was wrong. I just felt weepy and off. As mentioned above, I felt like I was different but couldn't figure out why. In grade five, my mental health took the biggest dive it ever had. I stopped trying at school. I started failing my classes. I was sad all of the time. I didn't talk to my family. I didn't play with friends at school. I was shutting down. My kind and compassionate teacher was at a loss. Where had the bubbly, eager, smart kid gone? Well, I was sick of pretending to be happy when I wasn't and I was even more sick of pretending to be "chill" when I was happy. I was tired. Life felt heavy. She arranged a meeting with my parents that I attended. They asked me what I needed to just TRY to do school. I just sobbed and sobbed and asked to go to the private school my best friend attended. I was so mentally and emotionally exhausted from trying to keep up socially that I had nothing left. My parents pulled me from the public system that year and sent me to a private school. There were eight students in my graduating class. The curriculum was clear and we progressed individually which meant I could go super fast in math and geography and take more time for spelling and reading. The teachers were the same, year after year and so were the kids. I flourished. Unfortunately, this school only went to the end of elementary, (grade eight), so I had to return to the public system for high school.

Heading into teen years, I wasn't too excited about anything really. I learned to mask even more in high school. I learned to be a wallflower. I learned to hide my joy and my sadness. My version of hiding quickly turned into sharp anger. I decided to be alone. I separated myself from my peers intentionally so that they couldn't do it to me. I still had my few friends and my church friends, but I didn't engage with classroom peers unless forced. Things began to feel heavy again in my school of 1,600 kids. Everything just felt so loud and exhausting. The cafeteria was absolutely out of the question, so I would usually eat lunch on the floor at my locker or in a classroom alone. Because a lot of my friends were older, we didn't go to school together. I always had headphones in, hoodie up, trying to escape the over stimulation. I didn't get why everyone else seemed so calm in what felt to me like super chaotic environments. I felt like I was on the brink of tears most days, but was unaware of what was causing it. The self-injurious coping continued and increased in severity.

I moved 14 hours away from my home when I was 23. I started over in a place I didn't know and I only knew one person in the whole province. That was so hard some days. It was around this time that I really started to question my neurology. I thought for sure I had ADHD, (I do), and started to live with that self-diagnosis. I made room for myself to be better based on not hiding my need for movement and engagement. About a year after that, I realized I'm probably also Autistic. I had worked in connection to the Autistic community for ten years at that point, (volunteering in special needs classes through high school/nannying/co-op placements/and later, jobs). I discussed it with two or three co-workers but wasn't sure if I wanted to know. After my health collapse in 2019, I moved back to Ontario. I began to discuss my thoughts on being Autistic with my brother and we decided I would seek out a diagnosis. That day changed everything for myself and my family. Being diagnosed as Autistic wasn't tragic, it wasn't even sad. It was affirming. It was peace giving. It was like I could breathe for the first time. I was seen. It made it ok for me to just be me. My family was much more in shock than me as I had known this for two years before I was diagnosed. I think at first it was hard for them to process. Probably some guilt for not knowing or for things that now knowing, they wished they would have dealt with differently. But now a year later, family life is so much better. Our communication is better. All of our individual (parents/siblings) needs are respected and not made fun of. We take into consideration others tolerances and preferences. It's been really great for our family culture.

So I get that that all seems super heavy. But my story is also full of love and hope and life. Let me show you that too. I am thankful for my childhood. There's definitely things I would change if I was magic. I would have taught myself to love earlier. I would have given my parents the tools they needed to support me well—they just didn't know what I needed. I would have learned to advocate for myself. I would have made sure I was seen and heard. Above all else, I would have had my parents understand me. But aside from that happening magically, I wouldn't have changed it, because let's be real, if I was diagnosed as Autistic 20-25 years ago, my life would be very different and I don't think for the better. I am pro-diagnosis now. But not then, not before we knew what we know now, and we aren't even close to done learning.

I'm thankful I wasn't in ABA 25 years ago. I'm thankful I was pushed to perform well academically. I'm thankful a label didn't ostracize me socially; I believe that would have been worse than just being the kid. I'm thankful for parents who loved and protected me passionately. I'm thankful for a mom who really tried—dragging me to specialists to figure out why I couldn't run around like a kid without dislocating an elbow or knee. For stopping the dentist when I couldn't take it anymore. For advocating the best she knew how. I'm thankful for a dad who patiently sat at the table for hours trying to teach me the deep "whys" in my school lessons, knowing if he could give me the "why," the information would stick. I'm thankful for my dad's knees, always available for a rest, to just hide away from the chaos of the world. I'm thankful for parents that became more concerned with my voice and needs than the opinions of their peers. I'm thankful for big brothers that read to me night after night when I struggled to keep up. I'm thankful for brothers that punched boys in high school hallways. I'm thankful for friends that loved me for me and all my weirdness. I'm thankful for friends that just smirk when I rock in the car because the song is on point or friends that aren't too cool to splash around with me when we go swimming. I'm even thankful for my trauma, because without it I don't think I'd advocate so passionately for the next generation. My experiences created deep empathy and compassion for other kids who need to be seen and heard and understood and after all those things, to be fully loved. That's what we all want, right? To be fully known, and fully loved.

So what now? What's life like for an Autistic diagnosed in adulthood? It's pretty great. I've worked for over a decade in child and youth care in dozens of different styles of environments. I've been a foster mom to three teenagers with FASD. I've been an ABA therapist for early Autism intervention, (I won't do this one again). I've been a behaviour technician working with kids with severe trauma histories. I've worked with deafblind young adults, basically making sure life was a party. I've worked in group homes and residential treatment sites. I've done parent training and child advocacy. I've been a nanny and I've homeschooled. Right now, I run my own weekly video segment designed to give parents tools to parent their kids intentionally and with deep love and dedication.

I believe with every fiber of my being that I am specifically and intricately designed with a purpose. I am not broken or defective or inadequate. I am not of inferior intellect or ability. My brain is wired to process sensory information differently, so I have a different life experience than what is typical which means I communicate differently. I move differently. I like weird stuff. Due to the boxy and controlling nature of our culture, these things unfortunately can be disabling. I am passionately working to change this. I believe in fighting for a world where we can function differently and provide equal value to one another's lives in different ways. I'm fighting for a world where Autistic and neurotypical people are seen as different and equal, like boy and girl.

James P. Wagner

James P. Wagner (Ishwa) is an editor, publisher, award-winning fiction writer, essayist, historian performance poet, and alum twice over (BA & MALS) of Dowling College. He is the publisher for Local Gems Poetry Press and the Senior Founder and President of the Bards Initiative. He is also the founder and Grand Laureate of

Bards Against Hunger, a series of poetry readings and anthologies dedicated to gathering food for local pantries that operates in over a dozen states. His most recent individual collection of poetry is *Everyday Alchemy*. He was the Long Island, NY National Beat Poet Laureate from 2017-2019. He was the Walt Whitman Bicentennial Convention Chairman and teaches poetry workshops at the Walt Whitman Birthplace State Historic Site. James has edited over 60 poetry anthologies and hosted book launch events up and down the East Coast. He is the National Beat Poet Laureate of the United States from 2020-2021.

Chapter 11: "He's Autistic"

by James P. Wagner

"He's Autistic"

"What's that mean?"

"It means we have to temper our expectations of him"

This short dialogue changed the course of my friend, Mike's life. He was my best friend growing up. I knew him when I was in 8th grade soccer and when I switched from Catholic school to public school in 8th grade, we reconnected—it was a bit rocky at first, dealing with his specific brand of temper tantrums, but at the same time, part of the reason I was leaving Catholic school was because in no uncertain terms, I simply did not jive well with the other kids...or the teachers...or the administrators. Square peg in a round hole didn't begin to describe it.

Not that that first year in 8th grade was any better for me by any stretch of the imagination—I not only had to deal with the fact that the public school curriculum was far different than the Catcholic school curriculum but I had to deal with being the new kid, in the final year of middle school on top of all of that. I got into more fights than I could count, dealt with constant bullying and the teachers while attempting to be helpful, yet no one really knew me well.

But somehow that year was better because in Mike, I finally had a friend who could communicate on the same wavelength with me. See, both of us had suffered many of the same issues growing up, not the least of which being the school system constantly wanting to put a label on us. For my part, they had sent me for all kinds of testing, suggested medications, blood tests, IQ tests, etc. I probably only endured half of what Mike had endured in this regard because Mike's was overtly different, I was covertly different. That is to simply look at me or to talk to me, you wouldn't know about my differences right off the bat. With Mike, it was a different story and because of this, literally, his story was different.

He didn't officially get his label until high school. By that time, he had already, despite his issues, accomplished quite a few things—band member, honor roll, etc. But once the label arrived, these things seemed like they were viewed as an exception and almost beheld as a temporary thing that would soon correct itself.

Labels have power. I am not against labels, they are necessary. I do not blame people for having them—without organization and the ability to put things into categories, civilization would be chaos. It was inevitable that the labels would bleed over into how we classify people. People, however, are far more complicated than things. A label can help us give direction, show us we aren't alone, and help us to discover things about ourselves, but a label can also hurt or limit us, or put us neatly into a box and make us think we belong in that box and only in that box. Or worse, a label can make the people around us, the people who have the most influence over us, look at us a certain way, and if people around us look at us a certain way for long enough, eventually this starts to heavily influence the way we look at ourselves. This is what happened in Mike's case, from his teachers to his counselors to his own parents.

In my own case, I've sometimes dealt with the opposite, at least as an adult;

"Are you sure you're Autistic?"

"You don't ACT Autistic!"

"You must be only a LITTLE Autistic"

or the ever-wonderful "We all have a little Autism."

In my adulthood, due in part, I think, to my personal successes both socially and in the world of business, people find my Autism to be questionable because of the societal beliefs that Autistic individuals seem and behave certain ways that aren't always visible at first glance. Again, covert, vs. overt.

I managed to avoid the official label while I was in school, thanks in no short, partly due to my parents worrying I would be treated differently with a label and who also wanted to avoid putting me blindly on drugs, which I am very grateful for because many of those same drugs that were shoved down the throats of unruly teens during the 90's have actually resulted in things from drug addiction to short-term memory loss in people my own age—from my own school system and that could have easily been me.

Not having a label in school, though, didn't of course protect me from the sensory overloads—the momentary switch from normal sound levels to times it feels like someone cranked the volume up to over 200. It didn't change the overbearing lighting that makes you want to wear sunglasses indoors. It doesn't save you from the very often migraine level headaches. It doesn't stop you from the fixations or the need to stim in ways that most people consider "harmless, but weird." These are the personal things that alone in a cabin in the woods would still happen—still be a struggle. Interacting with the world differently is something we Autistic people do naturally. But there are many different ways in which we do so and we don't always have a guide in that regard.

One very simple truth that I knew very early on was that the normal work schedule was not something I could ever do long term. I had many jobs growing up—the first one in my dad's store from the time I was ten. I worked a slew of part-time jobs, sometimes multiple part-time jobs at once, but the idea of a 9-5 forty hour regular work week seemed unbearable to me for more than a few reasons. Not the least of which being the chronic insomnia and the fact it seems like I function on something closer to a 32 hour day than a 24 hour day. I also have periods of hyper-focus and productivity where I can work for several days straight and on the flip-side, hyper, depression-level laziness where I almost refuse to get out of bed for days at a time as well.

This made it become an absolute must for me to become my own boss and start my own business. I knew there was simply no way I would function long term on the typical 40 hour workweek at the same time every day. I needed my own environment where I could work when I was in a peak state to work and have the time and ability to not work when my head and senses were not in the game.

This is exactly what I have managed to do—having my own publishing business for the last ten years, being my own boss, and yet, I still manage to upset people by not working conventional hours—the world is becoming very monolithic and everyone expects everything the same way. But luckily as my own boss, I can simply say, "this is how I do business, take it or leave it." Most people take it when they realize they get the results—usually better results than they get elsewhere via the traditional way and thanks to my high and low bursts of energy, I've become efficient at producing a lot in a lot less time out of necessity.

The other benefit I've managed to take into my business is my ability to fixate and become obsessive.

Something that can be harmful in social settings works very well when trying to learn a task or everything about something that needs to be done. It's great for acquiring skills related to the field you are in and once I sink my teeth into a project, I plow through until it is complete. The opposite can also be true in the sense that sometimes when I lose all desire for a project, completing it is almost impossible, so the trick is for me to get through something while the interest still holds. (Isn't knowing thyself fun?)

There is that old quote from Einstein about judging a fish by its ability to fly rather than swim and I feel like society as a whole does this all the time. I might work differently than many other people, but I still get amazing results doing it through the way that works for me. I have projects in over a dozen US states and a handful of other countries and make a pretty decent living for myself—something that would have never happened if I had to do things the traditional way and also something that would never have happened, in my opinion, if I had been labeled as early as Mike had been and if the expectations of me were "tempered."

Below is a poem I wrote on the topic of Mike, which was originally published in a volume of poetry I co-edited entitled "Perspectives, Poetry Concerning Autism and Other Disabilities."

His Disability

His disability was your excuse,
His disability,
Was why you did everything for him,
After his father left.
Woke him up,
Made his bed,
Breakfast, lunch and dinner.
Did his laundry,
Ironed his clothes.
Cleaned, scrubbed,
Took a second job so he wouldn't have to work one,
Even though he's 24 and you're 65.
But he can't work, right?
He can't clean, he can't do his laundry,

He can't cook…

"He's Autistic! What do you expect?!"

What do I expect?

I don't expect anything,

But I remember.

I remember him in the marching band,

Playing that trombone with more

Enthusiasm

than more than half of his fellow musicians.

I remember his dramatic readings,

In English class,

Iambic pentameter flowing out of his mouth as naturally

As each breath.

I remember, in history, he never forgot a date, could name

all the presidents backwards.

In science class…they might not have left him handle the

chemicals anymore,

after that…unfortunate incident with the eyebrows,

BUT…he has the entire periodic table memorized.

Gym!!

When he got hold of the football,

Everyone,

Myself included,

Parted like the read sea for Moses,

No one wanted to mess,

We all stood out of the way, of THAT charge.

I remember his room, spotless,

I remember him cleaning, taking the garbage,

I remember him making his own dinner.

I remember him…being social…as best as he could.

I remember early in 8th grade, when he did wrong, you'd

punish him.

I remember later on in 8th grade…the punishments

stopped.

I remember in the middle of 8th grade,

When he would hum to himself,

And twiddle his fingers non stop, and not realize,

When the other kids were making fun of him for it.

I remember they, the teachers, couldn't handle

That he couldn't sit down,

For the entire period.

I remember that they were clueless concerning him, and

when

it came time for a convenient classification, a consistently

competent, yet callous teach aid uttered the possibility

"Maybe he's on the spectrum"

His disability, you say,

You proclaim…

Was his disability the reason,

He could calculate faster and in higher denominations

than our TI-83's?

Was his disability what put him on the honor roll,

Was his disability what got him more scholarships to

more colleges than our graduating class's valedictorian?

Free tuition,

Free dorm room,

Meal plan books, all bought and paid for in a package fit for

a king,

Before he set foot there only so you could tell him

"it's ok, you don't have to do this if you don't want to, you

can drop out."

So he did?

His disability.

So now, he sits in his room,

All day long,

And you make his bed,

Breakfast lunch dinner,

Wash his clothes,

Clean the bathroom after him

While he

Does

NOTHING.

Gaining fat, gaining weight,

On the computer,

Video games, 24/7

No friends to speak of

No responsibility, productivity,

Life to call his own?

What happens to him,

When you're gone?

Now that you've taken off his gloves,

Taken him out of the ring,

His muscles have atrophied,

No longer able to go ten rounds, with life.

Will he relearn all that you made him forget?

Or will it be KO in round 1?

I don't know,

But don't talk to me,

About his disability,

Because I remember,

What I didn't stop him from doing,

His disability,

You exclaim,

His disability,

Disability defined as what gives one a disadvantage

His disability

His disability

His disability...is...you.

As you can see from the poem, Mike was not a person who was incapable. Before his official diagnosis, he was a very accomplished individual. There are plenty of people who will say that projecting expectations of abilities on those who cannot is ableist and in some cases that is true. However in the case of Mike, his own history proved he had the ability, but when the expectations were lowered of him by others, his own expectations for himself went with them. Today, he works part time at Home Depot, and hasn't done anything with the many talents he was gifted with. This is a serious danger for many who live with Autism and it's a fate I am very lucky and grateful to have avoided myself—simply because my own Autism was a little more covert than overt.

There are basically two challenges to deal with when it comes to being Autistic—the challenge society creates for you and the challenges such as the overloads, the fixations, the headaches, and whatever else you would be dealing with yourself. I've seen how labels can harm you, but I've also seen how definition and knowing thyself, often labels required, can also be a big help in figuring out what is best for you. I don't know the answer to which is better, but these are two stories of two Autistic men whose lives ended up completely different, simply because one person's Autism was more obvious.

I can say one thing from my own experience—Mike was given his label before he had the chance to fully figure himself out and by the time my label came, I not only knew full well who I was but how I functioned. I was able to see the grooves and curves in my own personality and quirks, the ways in which I could fit in, and the ways in which I never would and it helped me carve out my own place. I think that simple fact, at least for me, is what made all the difference.

Acknowledgements
By Aidan Allman-Cooper

It has been an honor and privilege to have been not only one of the compilers of the book, but to have served as the editor and to also be a contributor. It has been an incredible journey to not only spend time to reflect on my own experiences with Autism, but to also read the multiple perspectives and stories. I truly believe that as a result of this book, a community was built that cannot be broken. No matter how similar or different we may be in our Autism as well as our life experiences, there is a common feature seen within all of us—diversity.

I first want to thank the contributors for courageously sharing their stories. Because of each of you, a person's life has the potential to be changed through your advice and story.

I also want to thank my co-compiler, Jessica Leichtweisz. She is one of the most talented people I've ever met and I am so grateful to not only have been able to complete this with her, but to become a good friend as well.

I wouldn't have been able to move forward with this book without the constant support from my friends and family. Thank you to my friends from Kean's Bronze Leadership Program in addition to the New Jersey Scholar Program for building me up when I needed it most.

Finally, I want to thank Fusion Academy—Morristown for helping me reclaim my life. I especially want to thank my former English teacher/mentor, Chip. Thank you for helping me find my voice again and for helping me continue on my own journey. Stay golden.

Acknowledgements

By Jessica Leichtweisz

I want to thank all of the contributors of this book who bravely and vulnerably shared their stories...

I love you guys. Your courage and determination to make the world a better place is humbling and inspiring.

I also want to thank all of my mentors who helped me become the professional I am today, especially Deidra King who provided me with the support and best professional training anyone could ask for early on in my career and Susan Sly who taught me how to start and run a business...

Deidra, I would have never stayed in this field if it wasn't for your commitment to my growth early on. Thank you for never giving up on me.

Susan, you believed in me before I believed in myself. Thank you. I would never have had the courage to start my business if it wasn't for you. I love you and will always be grateful.

Finally, I want to thank Aidan, my co-compiler who worked tirelessly to make this book possible.

Aidan, the fact that you have accomplished everything you have at eighteen years old amazes me. You amaze me. You have incredible things in your future. Good luck in college this fall. One day, I will look back and be able to say, "I published a book with him!"

Made in the USA
Middletown, DE
13 August 2020